The Author in Shuriken-do Kamae

SHURIKENDO
My Study Of The Way Of Shuriken

SHIRAKAMI IKKU-KEN

Paul H. Crompton Ltd
102 Felsham Road,
Putney, London SW15 1DQ,
England

First edition 1987

Reprinted 1995

© Copyright Shirakami Ikku-Ken 1985

ISBN No 0 901764 94 9

London: Paul H. Crompton Ltd.

102 Felsham Road, Putney, London SW15 1DQ

New York: Talman Company

131 Spring Street, New York, N.Y. 10012, U.S.A.

Printed and bound in England

by Caric Print Ltd,

Clerwood, Corunna Main,

Andover, Hants SP10 1JE

(01264) 354887

CONTENTS

The author with Roald Knutsen

INTRODUCTION
by Roald M. Knutsen

The author, Shiragami Ikku-ken *sensei*, comes to the very centre of his thesis at the beginning of his text when he writes: 'I feel keenly that *shuriken* and the ancient military arts are of profound importance'. He places this importance not only in the historical past but also in the context of the present day. When we read his text we find not just another book on the technique of combat but a valuable contribution to the fundamental understanding of the nature of the martial arts as art and not merely on the level of sports and competition.

It is odd that in the past twenty years or so the so-called 'martial arts' of the East, in particular those of Japan, should have spread and multiplied so much in the West and yet almost totally mis-represented and misunderstood by those who have so wholeheartedly embraced them. The paradox lies in the fact that *Judo, Karate-do, Aikido,* and much of 'modern' *Kendo* are not martial arts at all but can only be defined as martial sports, whereas the truly traditional *Bujutsu* or *Budo* arts are practically unknown outside Japan. War and its myriad institutions has been a preoccupation of mankind since he first appeared and, like it or not, it continues to dominate our lives. The classical *Bujutsu*, the product of the turmoil of warfare in mediaeval Japan, were the arts of self-preservation. As the Japanese political structure became more stable the character of *Bujutsu* changed subtly into *Budo* and many systems became martial ways to achieve self-perfection. It is important to realise the *Kobudo*, a term that embraces both *Bujutsu* and *Budo*, is distinctly different from the post-*Meiji*, quasi-martial, sport-orientated *budo* of today.

The study of *Kobudo* is fundamentally the study of the art of war. Do we study in order just to fight; or do we study it in order to avoid fighting through developing skills that may be a deterrent to a would-be aggressor; or do we go further and study these skills in order to overcome the shortcomings within ourselves? In the swordsmanship of *Kobudo*, possibly the most influential area, the first of these reasons is termed *satsujin-ken*. It is the use of the weapon or technique overtly to gain the victory by any means available. The second and third reasons are far more important for our moral understanding and here the sword is called *katsujin-ken*. The small blades of *shuriken* are here presented as *katsujin-ken* which is one excellent reason for the importance of this book to all serious minded *Budo students*.

1

Mao Tse Tung once wrote[1]: 'It is well known that when you do anything, unless you understand its actual circumstances, its nature and its relations to other things, you will not know the laws governing it, nor how to deal with it, nor be able to do it well... Unless you understand the actual circumstances of war, its nature and its relations to other things, you will not know the laws of war, nor how to direct war, nor be able to win victory'. The German military philosopher Clausewitz said[2] that 'it is analytical investigation of the subject that leads to an exact knowledge'. The great classical Chinese philosopher Sun Tzu opened his classic treatise on warfare with the statement[3]: 'War is a matter of vital importance to the State, the province of life or death; the road to survival or ruin. It is mandatory that it be thoroughly studied'.

A modern authority on the subject, Shelford Bidwell, comments[4] that the study of war 'must be objective and free from romantic notions of false morality'. My own masters feel that in teaching the forms of swordsmanship we must approach the subject from an entirely realistic point of view. At first we undergo a period of basic training in the chosen discipline and during this period we must do our best to leave the subjective attitude to technique and pass on to an objective stage. This early period of training the body is termed *gyo* and how long it may last very much depends on the quality of the teacher and the ability of the student. A really good master is sometimes able to shorten this *gyo* stage and combine it quickly with the following period of higher level study called *shugyo*, or 'austere' training. Constantly the student must keep before him the theoretical or actual reality of warfare. It is too easy in the subjective early stages to lose this feeling of realism under the sheer weight of physical technique; understanding only comes after the limited mastery of technique and the student is able to reach beyond these boundaries and become aware of a far wider and more rewarding field for his endeavours. This is the *Jutsu* stage.

Realism in *Budo* can be interpreted in three ways. The first is the meaning of a *kata* form in the sense of illustrating to the student exactly what is occurring and the aim or purpose of the technique: this way is for the artificial surroundings of the *dojo* where everything can be seen under the most ideal and controlled conditions. The second interpretation is that applied by a number of *kobudo* schools who hold that the practice of form should as nearly as possible simulate actual conditions on the field of battle: these *ryu* prefer to take their practice outdoors on rough terrain and on occasion to even make use of the equipment of former days. The third interpretation may or may not follow on the other two and that is the explanation to the student of the meaning of the *kata* form in terms illustrating the wider applications in the art of warfare; budo seen as *heiho*, or tactics, in point of fact.

It can be seen that the very nature of *kata* is open to a variety of constructions at different levels. At the lowest, *kata* can be seen as merely theoretical form that underlies the more practical application in free combat practice. When it is seen in this limited way then it is very easy to fall into the error of believing that since *kata* is only distantly related to real combat practice, at this level, then it is an anachronism that can be dispensed with. At a higher level *kata* can be closely related to the practice forms as a means of reminding students how weapons should be handled and the forms that illustrate the basic principles of each discipline. The degree to which this interpretation is taken and the frequency of *kata* training in relation to the normal 'free' practice will determine the rate of progress a student will make towards a deeper understanding. I am thinking here largely of Kendo where *kata* is usually practiced with the curved *bokuto*, or wood sword, and 'normal' *Kendo* with the straight bamboo *shinai* – two very different weapons. At a still higher level we reach the *kata* of classical *bujutsu* and *budo* where the whole essence of the theory is contained within the *kata* and there is often no such thing as 'free' practice. *Iai-jutsu* and *Shuriken* are perfect examples of this level. While the *ryu-ha*, or school, *bujutsu* is taught exclusively in the form of *kata*, even here there is another level to which only a comparative few initiates reach. Students of the classical *ryu* practice hard and the *kata* takes on a much more realistic air of actual combat compared to the slower and more aesthetically beautiful forms of the Tokugawa period. At this stage of training there may not be an *Uchidachi* (attacker) or *Shidachi* (defender) in the meaning of these roles in later systems, but forms in which either combatant can defeat the other. The highest level is that where the practice is actually in the minds of those taking part, where the physical exposition is one thing but the actual meaning is something quite different. This is the spiritual or intellectual aspect and it is the most important objective to training.

But there is a word of warning proposed by the present headmaster of one of the oldest *ryu* and that is that all too often there is an inclination towards the physical side of training. This must be carefully watched for and all training balanced.

Another aspect of the nature of *kobudo* and *kata* is the degree to which tradition is important. This may be the least understood aspect of all to Westerners and to some extent be taken for granted or overlooked by the Japanese *budoka* themselves. At my own present stage of *budo* I can perceive a deep relationship between *kobudo* and

3

Shinto beliefs. If this is so, and very many masters firmly state the fact, then the whole subject is peculiarly Japanese with few parallels in Western culture. Because this is a most difficult area for study does not mean that it should be ignored; the advanced *budo* student should try to understand because any knowledge gained will add immeasurably to his 'awareness' in general. We will return to this question later.

The greatest single influence on the development of military thought in the *bushi*, or warrior, class in mediaeval Japan was Sun Tzu's theory of warfare. In the late mediaeval Japan was Sun Tzu's theory of warfare in Japan from the late 14th century onwards and the establishment of definite schools of military thinking, chiefly taking the form of theoretical and practical studies, in exactly the same period. It can be argued that the increase in warfare both in scale and scope would stimulate a parallel growth in the study of war, but it is a fact that the establishment of systems for martial studies was certainly given encouragement by the Ashikaga *bakufu* and by many great lords. It was towards the Chinese military classics that the warriors turned for inspiration.

Sun Tzu's premise that 'war is the grave concern of the State; it must be thoroughly studied' gave military 'experts' of all degrees a golden chance for advancement in an age of conflict. The character of these very old schools must have a bearing on the nature of their teachings. We divide the classical *budo* period up into those *ryu* that came into existence before the end of the Muromachi *bakufu* and those that were created after this somewhat arbitrary date towards the close of the 16th century. In analysing the sources for these *ryu-ha kata* we have to distinguish between those styles that were sound enough to survive the period of intense warfare in the Sengkou Period, many of which remain in being until today, and those *ryu-ha* that still survive but were never tested on the battlefield. The same basic sources of inspiration may be present for both, but on the one side we have proven worth and on the other only theoretical value. We have to be careful not to criticise but to balance our judgement after considering the differing aims of bujutsu on the one hand and budo on the other. If we accept that the influence of Sun Tzu, or Sonshi as he is known in Japan, was very great throughout the mediaeval period, then we must find this influence expressed in *kata*. We may find, also, that the earlier *ryu* were more direct and unsophisticated, that their success was due to the paramount need for a practical system for conducting warfare in the Sengkou period. In this early period the aim was for speed and effectiveness rather than for the later attention to complicated rationale. We will find, too, that

4

the systems that survived the Sengokou period and many of their direct derivatives, were very highly regarded by the warrior groups, and that their secrets (or theories of the application of Sun Tzu's principles) were jealously guarded from outsiders even down to the present day.

Great importance is attached to the practice of *kata* in traditional training. Shiragami Ikku-ken makes this point again and again. *Kata* is the essence; it is the centre of true education in the Eastern way. *Kata*, although following closely prescribed lines, is not necessarily inhibiting, and, ultimately, creative realisation or understanding will be reached through the close study of developed form. The reason for the fundamental importance of Sun Tzu in Japanese military studies is because it has always been recognised that the *Thirteen Chapters* represent the fully developed theory of the art of war despite the fact that it was written during the Period Of the Warring States between 450 and 300 BC.

All educated Japanese thought was influenced by the Chinese classics but it was not in the nature of most warriors to spend long periods of time in philosophical studies, indeed the business of survival precluded this, and so the greater and lesser lords turned to itinerant experts who were everywhere welcomed and found eager audiences for their theories. Any knowledge that would give an advantage over neighbouring rivals was avidly sought. In classical China unsuccessful sophists met a swift if unmerciful end; the luckier ones waxed fat. In fifteenth and sixteenth century Japan, perhaps the same was true. However, the Japanese were ever a practical race. The business of the *bushi* was war and he was little concerned with moral argument but more with the basic question of survival, not only for himself but for his family or his *han* (clan). It was within strictly delineated confines that the different *ryu* developed and were established. Their teachings and later philosophies remained closely guarded secrets within these groups.

[1] Mao Tse Tung: 'Problems of Strategy in China's Revolutionary War', Dec 1936,
[2] Clausewitz: 'On War' Ch.II, 27. (Penguin Books) (?)
[3] Sun Tzu: 'The Art of War' Book I, 1.
[4] Shelford Bidwell: 'Modern Warfare' p 40.

The study of advanced swordsmanship formed the core of the practical application of Sun Tzu's precepts. The method of practice combat between two men was the way that these principles could be demonstrated and then applied to the wider field of generalship. This concept was not Japanese, either, it came from classical China. Since the purpose of such study was understanding the principles of warfare and since warfare was the prime concern of the state, then it follows that advanced study of the deeper secrets could only be permitted to the most trusted warriors within the group. Many *bushi* of all ranks made up the potential or actual fighting strength of the unit, but only a few were admitted to the inner secrets of something so pertinent to statecraft. This was prudent. Since this was a serious and physically arduous method of study it was a characteristic of the ryu to divide up the forms into series of kata that introduced the theory, then examined it in greater detail and applied it to the use of a variety of weapons. This also meant that there was a natural percolation of talented men through the levels so that dedicated swordsmen might be found to strengthen the unit by admission to the higher levels from time to time; men whose worth and potential trustworthiness had been tested by this severe but excellent system of training. In *kobudo* history there are records of men, who, having reached the inner levels, were found wanting and had to be eliminated in order that the *ryu* should remain pure or that its secrets should not leave the confines of the unit – great or small. In the sixteenth and seventeenth centuries such defections were jealously guarded against and severely dealt with, usually with death as the best solution.

This need for secrecy in such an important matter as the art of war is still reflected in the deeply serious requirements for admission to the *ryu*. These requirements are considered very significant indeed and in no way incongruous to modern times. The spiritual arguments by which men seek to justify or deepen most activities, especially those of such consequence, came chiefly from *Shinto* in its simplest and probably most primitive form. We can argue with some justification that the inner core of study of the Art of War remained carefully hidden within the confines of the family or clan unit; hedged by strict rules to prevent the sight or possible knowledge of these arts or their application escaping to the wrong quarters. Furthermore, if warfare between individuals or groups necessitated the secret techniques of the *ryu* being used then those skills must be used *à outrance* so that there would be no survivors who might carry away the special knowledge to others.

That wandering scholars who were not bound by moral loyalties existed, we can have no doubt. Knowledge of the art of war in such a troubled period gave a promise of victory and its spoils to men who more than frequently had little thought for loyalty but only for opportunism. Sun Tzu bases much of his theory on deception; in Japan the interpretation and application of this ran riot. It was mainly in the more stable areas that the expert warriors were able to establish the earliest *ryu-ha* that later on deeply influenced the development of Japanese military thought down to the present day.

An interesting line of investigation would be into the connections between various families or *han* as the great 'source' *ryu*, inspiring fresh systems to develop in other areas. If these *ryu* were such secret organisations as seems likely then the only possible way that their theories would inspire fresh interpretations outside the parent discipline would be through permitted contact with collateral families or groups. No one would lightly give away such military secrets. One feels that the itinerant strategists did not have a lasting effect on *kobudo* though their theories and stimulation may have encouraged a lot of the warfare in this troubled period. Their successors may have come more into their own once the war period finished and the more successful could found military academies that proliferated throughout the *Edo* period.

One aspect of these early *ryu* that is not widely known is that in several instances they remained apart from the politics of the period and were little involved in the warfare. Yet they were still highly regarded. Two such were the important *Tenshin Shoden Katori Shinto-ryu* and the equally famous *Kashima Shinto-ryu*. The latter style was originally closely associated with the small *Kashima-han* and it is recorded that its chief inspiration, Tsukahara Bokuden, took more than one hundred heads in battle during his active lifetime; but the active tradition in this *ryu* maintains that it remained unaffiliated to any group after the destruction of the *Kashima-han* by the Satake in 1573 and was the *ryu* of the Kashima *jingu*.

Mao Tse Tung has made it quite clear that to him the thorough study and understanding of the nature of war is the most important point for without such understanding we cannot combat war or wage preventive war. Additionally the understanding of the nature of war is required at all levels of command. Mao Tse Tung made Sun Tzu the core of his whole military philosophy. Armed strife is not a transitory aberration but a recurrent conscious act and therefore susceptible to rational analysis.[5]

The Way of the Warrior is hardly the Way of the Philosopher, even a military one.

Interpretations are needed to enable practical hard-headed men to understand in real terms the more difficult theories of wise men. Commentators have discussed Sun Tzu at great length down the centuries; some, like Ts'ao Ts'ao (155-220AD), King of Wei, are highly respected for their penetrating illumination of Sun Tzu; but nonetheless simple workable systems are needed to train men to act in time of need. The Japanese *bushi* were certainly realists and it is a well-known maxim in *kobudo* that there is only one true way to understanding – hard practice. In the political turmoil that characterised much of the troubled Muromachi period it was very necessary to have skill at arms and for the established or ambitious families to have men about them who were expert in *hei-jutsu*, tactics, and were skilful in commanding troops in battle. The pressure was certainly there to encourage the thorough knowledge of the arts of war as the alternative was the destruction of the group unit and the total annihilation of its leaders. On both the lower man-to-man level and on the higher group level the adequate interpretation of these arts had to be effective. The survival of the individual or the group was the stake. Through the process of successive wars and as the Sengoku period drew to its bloody conclusion, great generals had emerged in Japan; that these generals were considered experts in the art of war goes without saying, but all these generals were skilled in the actual use of weapons and gave official encouragement to famous experts of *bujutsu* to teach within their areas of jurisdiction. The very best of these experts, often men of good birth and high rank, gave personal instruction to their masters.

With the virtual cessation of warfare in 1612 and the establishment of the stable Tokugawa *bakufu*, a process of change, already to be detected in the later *bujutsu*, added newer and more philosophical elements to the earlier study of the art of war and gradually many of the later *ryu* became softened in their approach to the subject.

INTERLOCKING RELATIONSHIPS IN BUDO

If the moral strength and intellectual capacity of man were properly applied to warfare then there was a certainty of success, believed the Sun Tzu. The whole structure of the developed bushi class and in particular the structure of the elite *kobudo-ryu* was based on the ideals of *reigi*. This is a difficult term to define. It derives from the Chinese '*li*' meaning propriety, but carries with it the sense of relationships between ranks, standards of behaviour, respect, and above all an acceptance of discipline within the group or unit, whatever its size. The structure of the *kata* and the method of teaching is also linked to *reigi* in that while training the student in the principles of warfare, it also strongly disciplines the student and enforces close attention to the basic requirements of the exercise and the unconditional obedience to his seniors within the unit. The *omote-kata*, or opening series of forms within most *ryu*, particularly demonstrates this as it must be mastered before any deeper instruction is given. It is the test to see if the student is suited to the group and its obligations. The relationships in *budo*, other than the obvious ones of blood ties, are deliberately strengthened by means of moral codes of behaviour and the need for fundamental discipline in all military matters. The influences that are invoked to this end may be the fundamental ones of native Shinto, they may be the intellectual morality of Confucianism, or the contemplative intuitive morality of Buddhism, but in *kobudo* they are all brought into focus by the rational analysis of the art of war as expounded by Sun Tzu.

It is a commonly made statement by many of the greatest swordsmen that the sword is only worn as a symbol. As Tsukahara Bokuden *sensei* is reputed to have said in the second quarter of the sixteenth century: "It is to cut off the buds of vanity that are apt to spring up in men's hearts." The sword can be said to be a symbol of justice, of law and order. The ideal objective of war is to win with the minimum of effort; war is never to be undertaken thoughtlessly or recklessly. Only if the opponent cannot be defeated morally and actually by all other means should there be a recourse to armed force – 'then, and only then, should you use your fully trained technique to the full'.[6] We can argue, therefore, that even in the midst of violent ages such as the Warring States period in ancient China and the equivalent period in fifteenth and sixteenth century Japan the great military thinkers who, it must be noted, were also masters of technique in their own right, were propounding the doctrine of 'benevolence and righteousness' that underlay the practicalities of survival. Sun Tzu was the first to state these principles and has exerted a profound influence on all Eastern military thought ever since. The object of the warrior's study was not just the use of the *satsujin* sword of indiscriminate slaying and victory but the *katsujin* sword of inner mastery in order to achieve mastery over all enemies. Not to fight was the best course, but if fighting it must be, then do it swiftly and to the full. 'Weapons are ominous tools to be used only if there is no alternative'.[7]

One of the greatest modern swordsmen, Yamada Jirokichi *sensei*, wrote:[8] 'I think that real *Budo* can be reached through training to hold back your opponent's plans with your own stratagems; by attacking his thinking; through breaking his look (*ki*) with your gaze; and developing the ability to forestall your opponent through reading his intentions in the small changes to be seen in his face due to the action of his spirit. To try to grasp the Way with a Ken, or sword, is called *Kenjutsu,* therefore *ken must not be separated from kenjutsu. Though this is a general concept, the essence is mind (spirit) and secondly kata* (form or style). *The style is the use of the mind; the mind is the master of the style.*' Sun Tzu examined the qualitites that made up a good general and the faults to be looked for in opposing commanders. His dictum was 'know the enemy and know yourself'. Yamada *sensei* paraphrases this with his fundamental statement just quoted that if 'the style is the use of the mind and the mind is master of the style' then through the study of *kenjutsu,* or *kobudo,* we can come to understand ourselves and be able to recognise the weaknesses and strengths of others.

Continuing his discussion, Yamada Jirokichi wrote: 'For a man who wants to establish his spirit through the martial ways then it is true that for a swordsman his mind appears in his sword; for a gunman his mind appears in his gun; for a painter his mind appears through his brushes. If you consider that the style is first neglecting the mind then your movements and applications would become just mundane everyday habits and mechanical actions... If a man only learns *budo* for an individual fight then he is a fool because there are many mechanical weapons these days. He should think, rather, why he endures such hard discipline spending so much of his valuable time and energy in his study.'

The art of war requires deep study; through *budo* we can acquire this knowledge and through the philosophy of *kobudo* we can apply these principles to the wider issues of life. Yamada *sensei* taught: 'Do not start a job if you know previously that you cannot succeed. In *Kendo* also, you shouldn't attack unless you can deafeat your opponent completely, knowing his mind. A win without thinking is not a real win. The same applies to everyday society. A win by chance is not a real win.'

[5] Gen. Samuel B. Griffiths, 'Sun Tzu – The Art of War'
[6] From the principles of an important *kobudu ryu.*
[7] Li Ch'uan, a T'ang Dynasty commentator on Sun Tzu. (Trans. Griffiths)
[8] The teachings of Yamada Jirokichi *sensei,* through personal correspondence with Kato Urasaburo *sensei,* June 1975.

AWARENESS

Throughout this book Shirakami *sensei* stresses the importance of that quality known in *budo* as *zanshin*, or awareness. This is a term that is almost impossible to explain but can only really be understood through hard training and constant attention.

One of the objectives of the various *ryu* is to offer to their initiates the wherewithal for adequate warfare; the certain conviction that the teaching of the *ryu* will measure up to and overcome any emergency. Success or failure depends on many factors, of course, but the most likely avenue to victory from the moral point of view is a pure heart and a bright sword.

Forget confusion
Look into the enemy's eye
Without moving –
Polishing the heart;
This is the path of the sword.[9]

Sun Tzu wrote:[10] 'It is a doctrine of war not to assume the enemy will not come, but rather to rely on one's readiness to meet him; not to presume that he will not attack, but rather to make one's self invincible'.

Mastery of *kata* through long and hard training places the *budo-ka* in a position of great strength. The deeper teachings of the great masters enjoin a moral strength that will effectively restrain an inclination towards reckless action and those other faults to be avoided in a developed and sound character. Steadiness through knowledge and the certainty of ability to act should the occasion arise, this is the essential thing. A warrior trained well in the arts of war is constantly aware in times of peace. *Zanshin* is fundamental in *kobudo*. One of the Chinese commentators of Sun Tzu described this: 'The "Strategies of Wu" says: When the world is at peace, a gentleman keeps his sword by his side.'[11]

The *bushi* cultivated their sense of awareness to a high degree. There are several anecdotes on the subject quoted by Yamada Jirokichi in his '*Nihon Kendo-shi*' and one swordmaster pointed out that even in passing a tea cup or handling everyday objects the *bushi* was 'aware', often only using his left hand so that his right, or sword hand, was constantly free for action. The very act of *rei*, the bow to show respect, correctly executed, illustrates this point. Within the *Hasegawa Eishin-ryu Iai* (Drawing Sword) *kata* three of the high level techniques examine this very point of *zanshin* during the *rei*.

There is an incident recorded about the developed zanshin of Yamada Jirokichi when a young man: One winter's day when it was snowing heavily, Sakakibara Kenkichi, the 14th Headmaster of the *Jiki Shinkage-ryu*, was on the way home from visiting accompanied by Yamada-*san*. They came to the top of the steep slope of Kudanzaka when suddenly the thong of one of Sakakibara *sensei*'s *geta* broke and he stumbled – but instantly Yamada Jirokichi caught hold of his arm to support him. Not only did he prevent his master falling but at the same moment took off his own *geta* and placed it to his master's foot using his free hand. His instant actions were so close that the hardened *bushi* Sakakibara *sensei* did not have time to refuse his student's proferred shoe. Sakakibara Kenkichi, who was not noted for giving praise, was so pleased with his student's action that when they came home he gathered his *desshi* in the *dojo* and recounted the story – it is said that tears actually flowed from his eyes. He praised Yamada *sensei*'s *kiai* and *zanshin* as a model of what can be achieved.[12]

Here we have another example of the maxim 'to know and to act are one and the same thing'. The only way to deep understanding is through hard bodily training; then, and only then, will the intellect or spirit be able to take over an instant appreciation of a situation made and accompanied by unerring action. Constant sincere practice is the key to kata; it is the key to *budo*. Not just attention to the physical surface but awareness, or *zanshin*, in its widest meaning.

SPIRITUAL INFLUENCES IN BUDO

During a recent *shugyo* stay in Japan (Winter 1976) I made several small pilgrimages to the burial place of Tsukahara Bukuden *sensei*. One of the last of these visits enabled me to spend several hours calmly focussing my thoughts on the significance of *budo*. It is the intangible influences that are so important to proper understanding.

This great *bushi* lies in a hillside grave quite near the site of his *yakata*, fortified residence, in a small valley leading east into the low hills bordering on the shores of lake Kitaura. This is a quiet unruffled valley where nothing has significantly changed for hundreds of years, so near to the main road along the side of Kitaura and yet remote from the bustle and rush of present day Japan. That day there was no sound save the rustle of a gentle breeze in the tall bamboo and the dark pines to disturb the rest of that famous man. Just below the hillside is the site of the Bykoji Temple that has since vanished without trace but was here when Bokuden was alive. The only memory of that holy place are five gravestones, two of which marked the graves of members of his *kerai* -personal retainers – now moved up from their former site to stand near their lord. It was so peaceful that a cat that was sitting waiting patiently for an unsuspecting bird or fieldmouse to offer itself but too lazy to actually go hunting, was still there four hours later, basking in the warm Spring sunshine.

Here I felt the very essence of *Budo* spirit: a feeling, intense and deep within, that is a response to the purity of nature. The association of this spot with one of the greatest swordsmen of all; the knowledge that it was his creative mind that inspired a profound understanding of the Arts of War, influenced many dozens of men down the following centuries, and continues in his spirit to guide and bring together the martial action and intellects of *budoka* who are in tune with such matters, is truly to be felt. It is not difficult to feel, even to see, that Tsukarahara Bukuden actually walked or rode through these same fields from his *yakata* on the next hill with his many retainers. There is nothing at all strange in the feeling in Kashima village that this warrior is still present, though long since dead, because his spirit, his soul, is undoubtedly near this spot.

In the Kashima *dojo* this sense of continuity is profound. It cannot be denied. Constantly one feels that the swordsmen of the *ryu* are in communion with this lord. This bond is mirrored in the family descent of the headship but it goes even deeper for the Urabe family have been ritualists at the ancient Kashima shrine since it was founded. They must indeed go back to the so-called Age of the Kami when the earliest and most primitive Shinto beliefs were just forming out of the chaos of folk-memory from ancient China and the keenly felt impulses from nature in a hostile border land – part real, part fancied. I think that there is a very signifciant connection between the blood relationship of the 'ritualists' at the important *jingu* and the fact that so many of these original swordsmen sought their creative inspiration by spending long periods immersed in Shinto in certain shrines traditionally connected with *bu*.

I don't think it is possible for the layman who is outside the *budo* environment to comprehend how deep the Shinto influence is in classical swordsmanship or the associated disciplines. I think this is something a sensitive person might feel but not truly understand without long years of severe training that are a necessary introduction. As Shirakami *sensei* so often points out, we cannot hope to understand *bugei*, the martial

13

arts, without undergoing the physical hardship of training. This has to come first. The body must be able to 'do' before the spirit can take over. There is no easy path.

It is also my opinion that the way of Zen in its contemplative form may train the spirit but it is not the path to try to follow from the start of a *budo* career. It is noticeable that the great *budoka* who enjoin the way of Zen have themselves followed the hard course along the 'wheel' of *bugei*. None of them so far as I know have started from Zen but all have come to it later. By the same token an equal number or maybe the majority remain under the influence of Shinto with its ancient emphasis on purity of body and mind. The symbolism of this simple belief is to be found in almost every true *dojo*. In some the very preliminary acts of cleansing the *dojo* and washing the hands before practice are in accord with the basic feeling of Shinto. Whatever the later influences in *budo* and howsoever these influences are given form, official or other-wise, the truth lies historically in early Shinto. Zen Buddhism and Confucianism only enable the more philosophical to give expression to the morality of classical *budo*. They are convenient articulate vehicles to express what is intuitively felt by Shinto.

This is something that is expressed in the *waka*:
Tall waving bamboo
By this peaceful hillside grave;1
Soul of Bokuden,
Following the sword's long path
Guiding true each hand and spirit.

It is the essential meaning, too, that the modern Japanese poet and calligrapher, Oda Tetsusaburo, has felt when he uses the symbolism of moss on this ancient world. Here is the state of no-mind of Zen but also the purity of Shinto. To me this purity is not of one man but its continuing influence down the centuries on many men who in their turn have each in some measure added to and enriched the tradition. Despite modern discord the truth of *budo is like the tall bamboo, giving way, avoiding, but never falling, always ready to spring back just as before. This same principle lies at the heart of true kobudo.* You cannot reach this understanding without hard training. It is *bunbu ni hiidete – bujutsu* and knowledge are the basis of authority. It is this perfection that Yamada Jirokichi points out as characterising the great swordsmen of the beginning of the Edo period and it is this that we should strive for in our own *Budo*.

In *bujutsu* this inner feeling is instinctive and so it must be if it springs from accord with Shinto. Zen has the same message but *satori* there is not drawn from the basic commune with nature but rather from an aesthetic development of understanding.

14

Shinto is a more primitive response, I am sure. I am equally convinced that its influence is far deeper in the simple hearts of real *budoka* who may not be able to understand the meanings of Zen. It is for this reason that many *Budo sensei* enjoin '*act, don't think*' as a basic principle of early training. Too much thinking or theorising creates imbalance and hinders advancement; even prevents it.

Many years ago I read an account of a visit to the birthplace of Miyamoto Musashi by Kondo *sensei, a Kendo Hanshi*, and even in translation I had a strong feeling of the tranquility and inspiration that this master had experienced on that day. Others who read the article felt the same. To understand something of these intangibles you must approach *budo* with a simple receptive mind; the mind of a child is how Yamada Jirokichi puts it, taking in everything but not necessarily analysing until experience tells you what should be done and when. To understand these matters we need to find excellent masters who in themselves will not actually teach but will show the way, the narrow and difficult path to knowledge through hardship, privation, and harsh self-discipline. Do not try to run, just spend time learning how to walk first; later we can run. There is no way to actually teach what *is budo* except in the early stages of physically imparting technical moves. Knowledge of what *is budo,* what *is* the essence of a style, the *gokui* or secret truth, can only be reached by the student through his own sincere effort. The master knows how to help this process; the student can only stumble on in the dark occasionally seeing the light of day. If he trains properly h e will reach *gokui.*

This feeling for physical and metaphysical influences develops a strong sense of respect. It is, at base, a respect for the natural laws that control *budo* and life itself. *Budo* is largely self-discipline; respect or *reigi* is discipline in all relationships within *Budo.* Respect for one's master, respect for his masters, respect for the *dojo*, respect for one's fellows, respect for the sword, and above all respect for what the sword represents. *Reigi* is the keystone of *budo* and I doubt whether it can in any way be separated from Shinto in true *bugei.* If we can to some degree understand these influences then we can grasp the concept that by respecting a master who may have long passed away, like *Bokuden sensei*, we are in fact still being taught by that master. There is a deep sense of continuity in real *budo.* Masters may be dead but their spirits remain reflected in the teachings of their successors. *Reigi* is vital if we are to achieve mastery. This is Shinto – this is *budo.*

9   Kobudo *waka* (poem), trans. Jeff Dann.
10 Sun Tzu: VIII, v 16.
11 Ho Yen-hsi, an early commentator about whom nothing is known (Griffith).
12 Kato Urasaburo *Hanshi* in personal correspondence.

Chapter one

MY STUDY OF SHURIKEN-DO

The *shuriken*, it is usually thought, is thrown by holding a *kozuka* (a small knife often found in a sword sheath) upside down. This is the only technique that is commonly known, although blade throwing is often described in stories and seen in films.

I am one of the few people interested in *shuriken* and have been since my boyhood. I feel keenly that *shuriken* and the ancient military arts (*kobudo*) are of profound importance; but nowadays, as with traditional *Bushido* (chivalry) they are dying out. I think it is significant to note the *shuriken*'s origins, technique and spirit. In the act of throwing a knife, there are expressed ways of thinking and living which reveal customs peculiar to Japan. By mentioning these, I would like to help you understand that the shuriken is still alive in the present.

As I take up my pen I think of my former teacher, Naruse Kanji, an amiable person who left his will to pass the art correctly on to posterity. It will be an unexpected pleasure if my aim is appreciated and used as a wisdom of life today.

THE TEMPTATION OF SHURIKEN

From the time I read the book "Fuji-Ni-Tatsu Kage" (A Shadow of Standing on Fuji by Shirai Kyoji) I was influenced by shuriken. This story features a man called Ueda Sanpei who first appeared in the book as an extraordinary boy of about ten years of age who was skilled at throwing stones. He gradually improved his technique, called himself Seitaken Sanpei, and became the best master of *shuriken* art of the time. He was head of a large *Dojo* where there were many students. There is an anecdote in the book in which the *bushi* Yonehara Kochiro visited Sanpei and was very surprised at

Sanpei"s skill. "You! Draw out a *torimato*" (a bird-cage target), said Sanpei to a student. "Yes, sir, which *torimato* shall we bring out?" came the reply. "Muremato will do." "Yes sir."

His students went quickly off to one side and they drew out a cage which seemed to have wooden wheels fixed to it. It was tipped over in front of a target bank and it made a creaking sound. In the cage there were several birds flying among the branches, and since Sanpei had called it 'muremato' it seemed that anyone would be lucky to get a hit!

"Master, we have set the muremato!" Sanpei nodded, took out a new shuriken, looked hard at the cage and muttered, "I"ll knock down the red bird in the cage."

Everyone could see that birds of all colours were mixed in the cage and that the red bird was flying about amongst them. "How will you do it?" asked Yonehara Koichiro with surprise. The bird did not stay still for a moment; it was surrounded by other birds, and, for good measure, the cage was covered by a net. Seitoken Sanpei was rumoured to be the greatest expert and most skilful *shuriken* master in the world . Yonehara Koichiro watched him with clenched fists. Sanpei took aim, indeed this time he could not get a suitable opportunity to strike even with all his heart and body. At last he raised his arms and stepped forward a few steps. "Ya!" he shouted and that same moment, a bird fell down in the cage. It was the red bird. Yohehara Koichiro could not refrain, despite himself, from exclaiming aloud in admiration.

I was still a boy when I read this book and I nourished the hope of becoming a master of *shuriken* like Sanpei. I had always enjoyed throwing things; it seems to be one of nature's primitive instincts; but there are not many people who seriously continue to practice throwing for thirty years. There was a knife, a pencil, a drawing pin, a nail, a needle, and a shoe-horn which I thew in my childhood. In addition to those I was particularly interested in throwing a *kiri*, or gimlet because I found that I could not make an ordinary knife or a nail stick from over two metres distance in full, but that when I used a gimlet I could stick it from five metres distance when using an underarm throw.

One's feeling when the object sticks into the target with the sound 'gatsu' is so exquisite that I cannot put it into words. It is one that seems to take over my entire being. At the moment that I make a satisfactory hit and hear the sound of 'gatsu', I feel that the power expended in throwing the blade flies back to my hand like lightning. Even if I throw the blade several hundred or thousand times, as long as I get a satisfactory hit, I do not feel tired. On the other hand, when I cannot hit correctly or, it makes a shapeless sound, I feel that the whole time I have spent throwing up until now has been absorbed into the eternal distance and I get very tired. Curious indeed!

When I was twelve or thirteen years old, I came home from school and threw a gimlet at any target until dark almost every day. When the weather was fine, of course, I trained in the garden; but, even if the weather was bad, I continued in my play house in the corner of the garden. At first my parents were worried about me because I was too enthusiastic, but eventually they gave up. I was a boy who wouldn't work hard at school or at other things, but I was enthusiastic about throwing a gimlet. After I gained confidence in myself in the way of throwing a gimlet, I could no longer throw an ordinary knife in this way or at least, I found it a very difficult thing to throw the knife. When I threw an ordinary knife from four metres distance, it turned round and round and wouldn't stick in the target as I wished and was very difficult to control. After that I noticed that it was fundamentally impossible to throw a knife which was not made to be thrown. Unable to throw a knife well, I was sometimes frustrated, but I did not give up. I was sure that there was some secret knack. I want to make it clear that my desire became even stronger, but that I thought my training wasn't going well because I only had an ordinary knife. So I hunted secondhand shops and asked if they had any *shuriken*. By chance, there was a shop in Shibuya that said they had some. I was surprised when the shopkeeper brought out a *kozuka*. Of course I knew about *kozuka*, but the shopkeeper was confident that it was a *shuriken,* so I bought it. I've forgotten how much it was; I just remember it cost me all of my pocket money. At last I had gained a real throwing blade. I used it carefully, trying to throw it at a board target. As with the knife, I couldn't make it stick at first, but gradually I got used to it and could control it. At long last the *kozuka* stuck in the target, but at that moment the top of the *kozuka* came off. Heavens! It was too late.

At this time I was doing *Kaitendahō* (the way of the turning hit) in my own style, because I was thinking of turning a gimlet between me and a target. But this way of throwing was only effective from a distance of three or four metres and was uncertain. It was a long time after that I learned the secret of the turning hit; "The turning of a blade should not be done closer to me than the target; throw it to turn just before the target". I also learned that we should use a straw mat as a target. My strongest wish at the time was to learn the *shuriken* art my any means, to make a hit with a blade as I wished, and to gain confidence in *atari* (a hit). I also had to prepare for the high school entrance examination at this time but I was more intrigued by the secrets of *shuriken* than by preparing for the examination. All I thought about was mastering the true *shuriken art*.

MY INTRODUCTION TO SHURIKEN

The first time I saw that true *shuriken* art was while I was preparing for the high school examination. By chance, an association for the promotion of the classical military arts of Japan presented a display of the martial arts at the Meiji Shrine on the day of the Meiji celebration (3rd November). There was a display of the *shuriken* art of the Negishi-ryū amongst the Kenjutsu of the Yagyu, the *sō-jutsu,* or the spearmanship of the Hozoin-ryū, the *kusari-gama-jutsu,* or the art of the sickle and chain, and the *jitte-jutsu, or art of arrest. That day I learned that there existed a man who practised the true art of* **shuriken**, and I saw the proper way of throwing blades. I was surprised also to see a woman who threw the blade. As I had been thinking that it was difficult to attain the real *shuriken* art, I hadn't considered the possibility of seeing a woman there at all.

My next surprise was that a tassle was fixed to the blade stuck in a target, the tassle opened like a blossom in bloom. As I later found out, this was the blade of the Negishi-ryu.

The demonstration of the *shuriken* art was Master Naruse Kanji. His *kamae* (position) was completely different from my own. The woman swordsman also threw a blade in the same *kamae*, so I suppose that that way of throwing was the *kata* (form) of *shuriken*.

My next surprise was that a tassle was fixed to the blade stuck in a target, the tassle opened like a blossom in bloom. As I later found out, this was the blade of the Negishi-ryu.

I could hardly sleep that night because of my impressions and I even saw the white thread tassle opening in the dark as I dozed. After that display of the martial arts, I re-dedicated myself to learning the true *shuriken* art.

I visited Master Naruse on a warm day in the mid-summer of the following year. I met him and asked point blank: "Take me as your pupil, please." But the master gave me a flat refusal. He said, "There have been many people who wished to learn but there has been hardly any who accomplished it, because it is so difficult to attain. No doubt you will be the same, and since this is not my occupation, I have no intention of taking pupils."

But the master was softened by my begging to have him teach me. He said, "Well, then, since you have come all this way to see me, I'll show you a real *shuriken*." I was taken to the gymnasium of the school by his house and I learned that this school for the deaf and dumb of poor families was run by the Master and his wife. The gymnasium was upstairs and contained about thirty straw mats; and being also his *dojo*, it had a target fitted up in one corner. Here, for the first time, I held a real *shuriken* in my hand. In addition to the shuriken with a tassle, there were many other kinds. In asking about these, I forgot my fears; perhaps the master might think I had a chance. He gradually gave a fascinating explanation, and taught me the basic form of the way of throwing in the Negishi School. Just before I left his house he gave me a *shuriken* and said, "I'll give you this so you can try to throw it at home as I have taught you." It was a blade with a tassle. Ever since, I have looked up to Naruse *sensei* as my master.

1. 1. Koso no I of Master Naruse.

STRAIGHT TO THE SECRET

Thus I had been given a *shuriken* by my master, at last I had taken a step towards the true way of the *shuriken* art. My purpose had definitely been decided, the days of training without knowledge were over. I had to prepare for my entrance examination to high school, but my mind was full of dreams about *shuriken* and I gave every spare minute to training. The ground between the target and myself had been stamped down like a shallow gutter by my going back and forth several hundred or even a thousand times. The target of *shibuita* (board of 1.2 cm thick) was full of holes and had fallen to pieces.

When the tassle of the blade which the master had given me had worn out, I inspected it. There was a hole at the tail through which to pierce ten strings. The strings were collected and fastened there and were wrapped by other strings. At first, I even didn't wonder why the tassle was fixed there, but I found out why, after I had trained and renewed the tassle often. As a tassle wears out and get shorter, a blade flies a long distance; and then as the strings wore out over the limit, it won't even fly a short distance. I eventually found out that a blade with a tassle is for a beginner, and the proper one has a short bunch of horse hair at the tail of the blade.

After one month had passed since my first visit, I went to see my master, and this time I had some confidence in myself. After I was taught the ritual towards God and the target, I at last had to throw a blade in front of my master.

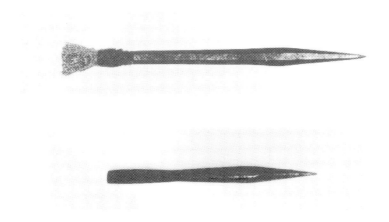

The day before I had been able to hit well from a distance of three or four metres but as I stood in front of my master, my body and arms stiffened and when I threw a blade it turned and fell down under the target with a shapeless sound. I was disappointed with the thought that the master would scold me and say that if I was like this I was incompetent to learn *shuriken*. Whereupon he looked as if this was quite in order, and he didn't care at all that I couldn't make a hit with even one blade. He said: "You have trained a lot! Even though you couldn't make a hit you mustn't lose the right form. Take it more easily and throw it at one pace forward." As he spoke I took a step forward, relaxed my body and arms, cooled myself down and threw it. The first time I struck the target with a pleasant sound; and strange to say, after one hit my stiff body relaxed and I could make a hit one time after another.

As I look back at it now, I see that I put too much force in my body, and that the idea that I wanted to hit well overcame my understanding for distance (*maai*).

I went to my master's house every ten days and learned the technique of the Negishi-ryu step by step. It was very difficult to leave the mind "not stiff", "not to wish to throw well." Afterwards, what I gradually understood was that we cannot separate or cut off these senses (we mustn't be stiff or be nervous), because as a human being we take it for granted that the mind will stiffen naturally in a case of emergency. Bearing this in your mind you just continue the training to be able to let go without tension. The more you train the more you will feel free from the senses. A blade correctly directs itself if we do not interfere.

The training was very severe and although my master didn't raise his voice at me, it was a period of continuous tension. In a large *dojo* the master and his pupil threw blades into the void for several hours at a time. The boy whom it was thought would stop coming after a few visits continued to come; and it seemed that my master was beginning to believe my seriousness. I have been a sticker-at-nothing but this, anyway we do not make something we like last out?

I had got into the habit of looking after myself since I had an attack of light pleurisy at the age of fifteen. Even when I was in the depth of training a corner of my mind was occupied by the anxiety that I might have a second attack of pleurisy and come to the point where I would not be able to throw a *shuriken* again. But in the end I came to think that even if I fell down during my training I should still be perfectly happy. The point which I had reached in my mind could be expressed thus: "I am quite willing to die on my way" (*ware, michini shisuru o itowazu*" from *Dōkodō by Miyamoto*

Musash).

I FORGET MY EXAMINATION

The other students of my age were pushing straight forward to the entrance examination. I was thinking that I had to do the same, but "the fascination of *shuriken*" was stronger and carried away my mind. Saying that I would cool my tired head for study or for a change, I trained in a warehouse; but once I started to throw I ended up throwing for two or three hours in spite of myself. Thinking about the way the blade was thrown and stuck, the time when I walk to fetch the thrown blade is "an artless state" which I can not explain. Even though it would seem a waste of time to other people, for me every hit was a different 'creation'.

During the struggle I felt as if an idea had flashed across my mind and I had been able to attain to some new state. The pleasure, it is something I cannot express in words.

Since I have mentioned how I came into the way of *shuriken*, I will relate how Master Neruse came into the way, as I heard the story.

A CHOPSTICK STUCK IN A STRAW MAT

The Naruse family was originally the head family of Iai-jutsu (the art of drawing a sword) of the Yamamoto-ryū which was handed down by the Kuwana-*han*. Master Naruse had trained in the way of Iai-jutsu and had a profound knowledge of swords themselves. During a war with China he gained some experience of sabre-fighting and he later wrote a book on "Japanese Sabre Fighting" in which he mentioned his experience at the time. When he was doing research he happened to meet Master Tonegawa Magoroku, the last successor of the traditional *shuriken* art, and it was thus he entered this way.

It happened that on the 15th of April, in the second year of *Showa* (1927) there was a meeting at a Miyama Club at Denma-cho, Yotsuya-ku, Tokyo, in those days. It was a heavy, snowy day out of season. It was the first time that Master Naruse had been able to listen to the story of *shuriken* as a Martial Art.

Tonegawa was an aged man who was born into the *bushi* family of Kanbayashi Joshu. He had trained in the Martial Arts from his childhood, especially *ken-jutsu*, swordsmanship, sō-jutsu, spear art, and *ba-jutsu,* horsemanship. During the Meiji Restoration he went to the Aizu battle (1868) at the age of eighteen. After that he served for Gunma provice as mayor or some towns where he rendered distinguished service. In his old age he was leading a life of ease and contentment at Sendagaya, Shibuya-ku, as an advisor to Viscount Akimoto.

The audience listening to his speech asked him to demonstrate. The old man sharpened a chopstick with a knife and threw it at a straw mat. It stuck so well and deep that all present were very surprised. But the man most fascinated among everyone present was my master, Naruse. After two days had passed, he visited the old man and asked for admission as a pupil. At first he did not give admission, and said, "Entering the way of *shuriken* is hard and attaining perfection is not easy. Up to now I have initiated more than one hundred people into it, but none of them accomplished. Perhaps you will be the same. You and I will come to nothing." But Tonegawa was at last moved by his enthusiasm and agreed to take him as a pupil. For thirteen years he learned under his master until the aged man left this world on the 7th of February, the 14th year of *Showa*, (1939), at the age of eighty-nine.

KANIME-NO-DAIJI (EYES OF A CRAB) – A MATTER OF IMPORTANCE

On the 1st of December, the 18th year of Showa, (1943), all university students throughout Japan who had reached a certain age were drafted. I had to serve in the army as part of the first formation of '*Gakuto Shutsujin*' (students going to battle). The tide of the war was turning against us, and we had a presentiment that we would be the last line of attack.

On the 15th November when enlistment into the Tōbu (Eastern) 12th Unit in Setagaya Tokyo was approaching, I went to the *Dojo* of my master to receive the last teaching of the way of *Shuriken*. This completed, the Master Naruse sat straight at the centre of the *Dojo* and said; "Today I'll initiate you into the secret of '*Kanime-no daiji*', which is the last secret of the Negishi-ryu. When you face an enemy and the final moment has come, rush in until the tip of your left hand reaches the enemy's sword, and look into the enemy's eyes. When the pupils of the enemy's eyes look as if they are jumping out like the eyes of a crab, thrust a sword towards the pupils and your victory will be decisive. If you cannot see his pupils, it is the time of your death. Stop throwing your *shuriken, and charge with shuriken* in each hand so that you pierce into his eyes and both of you die together."

Thus is the outline of 'Kanime-no daiji' as Master Naruse told it to me and he himself was originally told it by the aged Master Tonegawa.

Step-by-step training must have been mastered to perform 'Kanime-no daiji' completely. In order not to make mistakes at 3 steps in front of the enemy, we usually have to be well trained not to make mistakes at 10 steps or 20 steps. We need training in 20 or 30 steps for a possible 10 steps." A fountain in the garden springs up high, because the fountain-head springs from a high, far mountain." When the master said to me: "I'll initiate you into the last secret of the school", I expected to be taught the secret of the most correct way to hit from a long distance or the secret of making an elaborate sword, but what I was in fact shown was wonderful beyond all imagination. This was indeed the teaching which expresses Japanese *Bushido*. The final point to which I had come through the hardship of the problem of *maai* (distance), and for which I had worn down my heart and soul was the teaching: "Do not throw the blade, fly forward and rush against the enemy with a *shuriken* in each hand, and die together. You don't throw a blade, you and the blade become one body, that is, you yourself fly like a *shuriken*." At the end the master gave me his dearest blade saying: "I cannot stand in the fore-front of a battle, but, in my place, serve our country with this blade."

There is a poem by Bukkoku Kokushi (a high Buddhist priest) of Ungan Temple, in Nasu, which I love to sing, and which expresses the state of this secret: "*Yumi-mo-ore, Ya-mo-tsukihatsuru tokoro-ni-te, Sashi-mo-Yurusa-de, Tsuyoku ite miyo*": that is: "The bow has broken and the arrows are spent whereupon shoot an arrow strongly without fear".

GAKUTO SHUTSUJIN

At last the young university students all over Japan had to go to the final battle, *Gakuto Shutsujin*, the last charge of Japan. Already, my classsmates had gone to battle one after another, day after day. Because I knew that each class might be my last, I listened with fullest attention. Students knew then what was meant by the expression: "Life is Twenty-five."

In early November, a farewell party was held in the upstairs room of a coffee shop near our university. I received words of encouragement from my teachers Fukui Yasumori and Kurita Naohiko who had always understood me, the youngster who didn't work hard at his lessons and only endeavoured to train in the martial arts. I left the school gate full of memories.

On the first of December I joined the Tobu (east) unit in Setagaya Tokyo. As this was a field artillery unit, I spent all day training to fire a gun and practising horsemanship. I was not interested in firing a gun, finding it too mechanical, but I endeavoured to learn horsemanship because I found it interesting. Before long, special training for military cadets had begun and I had no spare time to throw a blade. When we could manage to fire a gun, it was decided to send us to the southern battle line. By this time, the United States had command of the air and of the southern sea. We were cut off from the front, and every day we were bombarded from the air just like the man on the street in the centre of Tokyo. As I was calming down the horses, wild with fear of the bombs which fell like rain, I thought: "I am going to die, and without having had the chance to perform at the centre of the *Kamada* parade ground." At all times and places I carried with me the two *shuriken* which I had been given by my master.

In April, the 20th year of *Showa*, at last the war drew to an end. Our unit had moved to Itazuma on the lower slopes of Mount Fuji where we were surrounded by the primeval forest with Mount Fuji towering above. Taking advantage of a break in training I went off, and threw my blade at a nearby tree, the true feel of *shuriken*.

Our unit had moved to this location with the object of repulsing the enemy who would disembark at Sagami Bay. Ours was intended to be the decisive battle of the mainland. The decisive unit, however, was in a pitiful state. After a long diet of only Kaoliang rice, plantains and potato runners, the soldiers and horses were unsteady on their feet. Some horses were unable to stand unsupported, and were hung fron the ceiling in the stables, enabling them barely to stand upright. The outside of the soldier's sabres were made of bamboo and the military uniforms were the last that the Japanese army had. The shells were supposed to last for three days of battle, but a military officer was heard to say that they would be used up in a day. Such was the state of the crack regiment of the Imperial Field Artillery Guards.

We concentratred on training in short distance artillery fire. Learning to shoot the enemy at 10m, just in front of the muzzle, we were taught the art of self-destruction, told not to give the last gun to the enemy, and trained to use incendiary grenades and impact bombs on disembarking tanks. "One man, one tank", was the slogan.

This was indeed 'Kanime-no-daiji'. Still, I longed to be able to dash in with my *shuriken* for the last time. At least, my everyday use of *shuriken* would be well employed since I was outstandingly excellent at throwing grenades, and was promoted to be in charge of grenade throwing in my battery. At last, ' Kanime-no-daiji' was not a thing of the past but of the present; not only for me, but for all Japanese. But at that point the war ended, on the 15th of August, and I left the army with the *shuriken*s in my pocket without having thrown 'Ichida' (one hit).

THE LAST TRAINING

The war over, and I returned home in early September. I was attacked by tuberculosis and had to have one rib removed. Unable any more to throw a *shuriken* I was a sea of confused motion. After a few months, I brought myself to confront the target with a blade. Bit by bit my strength and self-confidence returned, and I longed for more training by the master, who at that time was living on a farm at Akitsu on the Seibu line, where copses and grass grew thick. Musashino was in its former prosperity. Though he was overjoyed when he congratulated me on my demobilization, ("At least you have come back alive"), I was aware of the gloomy feeling of one who faced the defeat of his fatherland as a military power. After a long talk I braced myself and asked: "Would you be willing to resume training me after such a long interval?" At that moment it seemed to me that his gloom vanished and his face lit up as before. "All right", he replied. He went out into the garden and put me a short distance in front of a big tree. As soon as I saluted the master and then the tree and positioned a blade, all my thoughts vanished. A long time had passed but I would throw the blade as I wished and there was not the strain or fanatic feeling I'd felt before the war. The master also coached me with an ardent spirit. The sound of the flying blade and of my own shouts echoed in the copse in the gathering dusk. There was the world of a sword which overcame everything. "This is the way to keep it", said the master to me, and we had completed my first training in a new era. When I left the house, he saw me off to the station and that was also my last training-session with the master, because shortly after that he fell ill, and at last, passed away. That last training in a corner of Musashino in the dusk became a precious memory that I have never forgotten.

SHURIKEN AND EDUCATION

After I was demobilised, I returned to the university and, after graduating, I taught at a high school for a while.

Wherever I looked, I saw my country ruined by the war and disordered by the new ways. I thought that I would some how like to play my part in Japan's recovery; so I became a teacher at the Jiyugaoka School for boys in Meguro. At that time I was so impressed by a book, 'Notice to the German People' by Fichte, that I really thought that present Japan would take on a new soul.

At the time, the policy of the educational authorities was uncertain. To me the most important questions were, "How do we help our country recover?", and, "How can I make the most of the spirit of Fichte in education?" By chance, I was in charge of social science subjects, centering around the history of the rise and fall of nations in all ages and all places. Always I emphasised that "the rise of a nation depends on the mettle of a young man's mind."

The general situation at the time was so decadent that the only thing that inspired anyone was the company of students. I was teaching against the grain of the situation as it was and I was surprised that the students listened intently to me.

Among one of the teachers' duties was to check the classrooms to see that everything was all right after school was over. One day I was looking around the rooms of the new school building when I heard the sounds of someone sticking something in a board. As I entered the room a student was throwing a knife at a wall, as my professional intuition had told me. "What are you doing!" The student looked back in astonishment. "Have you no shame that you throw a knife at the wall of the classroom?" I was shouting at the top of my voice, because it still seemed to me that a classroom was a *Dojo*, as before the war. The student apologised. He came from a good family, but was under observation as a hooligan who kept company with others

28

of that sort. He had great physical strength, and the hooligans respected him, though he did not fight. "You must stop acting like this", I said, and was about to leave, when I recalled that, though, he was usually so quiet in the classroom that nobody noticed him, when something destructive happened, he was usually found to be the ringleader. Taking a chance, I went back to him and said as I looked him in the eye: "It is bad enough to throw a knife at the wall of the classroom, but at least, if you really want to throw the knife, throw it in earnest. All things must be done in earnest, and in the right way. You should throw the knife like this – watch carefully!" Taking the knife I flung it at the wall: it had stuck more deeply than I'd expected. "You see? anyone can throw a knife, but it takes ten or twenty years to do it right." I left for the teachers' room leaving the knife where it was.

A few days later, he came after school to see me at the teachers' room. He had never been there before, so I was suspicious. "Teacher, will you teach me the correct way to throw a knife?" he asked earnestly. My reaction was: "Don't teach the martial arts to the evil-minded." I said, "As I told you before, only an honest person can throw a knife. Someone like you who doesn't study and is violent cannot throw a blade correctly, so I cannot teach you." He went away very disappointed. As I found out later, his response to my words was: "Learning has nothing to do with it. I will train hard and surprise the teacher."

He trained hard for a few weeks, but failed to get even one blade to stick. But he could not give up wanting to know how to throw, having already seen my technique. I had already forgotten about the incident when he came to see me again. "Teacher, I'll work hard and earnestly. Please teach me."

When I saw his face, I realised that he really wanted to learn. "Well, if you want to practice and learn in earnest, I'll teach you, provided you promise to use this skill only for good."

It is very dangerous to teach *shuriken* to someone like this boy, but I sympathised and identified with his quite genuine urge. I invited him to my house and began to teach him the basic form. It was an adventure and an experience for me. "Don't tell anybody that you are having lessons and don't show anyone where you train." I made it quite clear to him that if he broke his promises I would stop teaching him at once. In fact, he obeyed the order and trained hard.

He had never worked hard at his studies, so it was no news that he did not work hard in class. At home he made a target in a corner of his house, and could not wait to get home and pick up the blade. As I had done, he threw a blade all day when he was free.

I followed my master's teaching which was: "When you teach the martial arts, check to see if the site is suitable", and went to check his house a few times. There I met his mother. I later heard that his parents thought that I was a strange teacher indeed, teaching their son to throw a knife, and never telling him to work hard at school but instead coming to the house to encourage him to throw in earnest.

After a few weeks, I could see many changes in him. His scattered mind was concentrated on *shuriken* and all of his energy involved with it. He had no time left to see his dissolute friends. Up to this time he had thought that all teachers were disgusting people; but a feeling of gratitude and the knowledge that his teacher secretly taught him *shuriken* gave him a budding sense of superiority.

AN HONOUR STUDENT IN SHURIKEN

Even if knife throwing was not an education, the training brought about a big change in his mind. He began to have pride and a sense of his own superiority and I could even see some self-possession in his speech and conduct. He seemed to be a different person.

I often took him with me to a ravine near the Tama river and let him draw a bow at a target. In this case the target was me, for the purpose of the exercise was to look into the soul of "*Yadome-no-Jutsu*" which was handed down by the *Batenen-ryu*. "*Yadome-no-Jutsu*" was literally the art of receiving an arrow , which is flying towards one, with a sword. Ever since I had seen this at the great meeting of the ancient martial arts, I had wanted to try it. I coiled a wire gauze to a swordsman's mask and trained. We stood on the ground of the deserted ravine. He stood at a distance of 20m and shot at me. An arrow shot at one's face with a terrific whirr of feathers is really frightening. The moment that you try to catch or avoid it, you lose your freedom. I thought, first of all, that I had better throw away everything. I stopped having a sword, took the stand still posture, and let him shoot. Of course, I wore protective clothes and let him aim at my body. Gradually I lost the stiffness of fear, and after that I faced an arrow with a sword for the first time. I learned not to receive or avoid an arrow but to try rushing into the centre of the flying arrow with a sword. That way, the arrow definitely catches at the

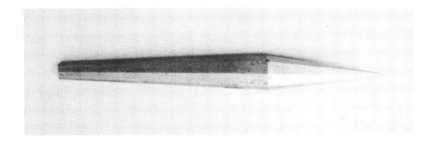

edge of the sword and naturally flies away to the right or the left. I can't explain this dashing into the flying arrow with the body and the sword. Of course, we did not often achieve success a satisfactory *Yadome*; but we continued to practise over and over again until we were tired out. After a time, I let him experience *Yadome*, and when he practised this he had completely changed. I suppose he felt that he was living in another world.

Thus there came about a deep spiritual exchange between the boy and me, through the means of a blade, a bow and an arrow.

If the device at the tail of a *shuriken* of the *Negishi-ryu* is scientifically looked into (especially aerodynamically) the results will be interesting. This would not only scientifically recognize and establish the greatness of our ancestors but might also be a good chance to develop a new design of *shuriken*. I often thought about this and one day I happened to mention it to the boy. It seemed to impress him very strongly and I realised how the words and behaviour of a teacher can have a deep influence. The boy then made up his mind to look into the matter scientifically. Until that time he had not decided what way of life he wanted to lead, but he made up his mind so finally after our talk that he had clearly found his way of life.

From that time he became a student who worked hard. To examine the *shuriken* scientifically, he had to go into the science course and had to work hard. Suddenly, though a little late, he was concerned about his school record. His parents, who had been very perplexed that a teacher was teaching their son such a funny thing, were amazed that through my training he became first a good boy and then a good student, and they were delighted. His training time at *shuriken* did not become less, but he studied in his spare time.

He completed the high school course and then entered an institute of technology. I suppose he studied physical science and engineering, but the most important thing was learning how to put them to use for his investigation of *shuriken*; he could learn the technique of making a *shuriken* in a way which our ancestors could hardly imagine. He worked away with a will and this enlarged his outlook so that gradually he took an interest in other subjects.

He went out into the world as a university honours graduate, followed his father and entered a pharmaceutical company and at present works as a capable engineer. Perhaps if I had not taught him *shuriken* he would have been an honours student in another course? Who knows? To me he is an example of *shuriken* deciding and changing the direction of a man's life.

AN EXPERIENCE ON TELEVISION

One day when I was living at Muko-ga-oka near the Tama river, a car stopped in front of my house, which didn't happen very often at the time. The visitor was a stranger, Mr Sasaki Ken, who was a well known historical dramatist. I wondered why a person like that would want to visit me. He said, "As part of a series of historical drama, we are presenting the play '*Doronko Hime*' starring Matsushima Tomoko. There is a scene in which a woman's sleeve is fixed to a sliding shutter by a *shuriken*. When we resort to tricks it lacks power, but when we tried to do it before the camera, it became a problem so we decided to look for a real expert and we happened to know about you from the Association of the Martial Arts. Please help us."

Never having had an experience like this I wondered what to do. But Mr Sasaki seemed to be in a fix and my experience being valuable I said, "Well, I'll try."

After that I found out that the scene was the most important part of the drama, so I began to train hard to pierce a cloak hung on the target.

At last the day came and I went to the studio in Akasaka. This was a good chance to look around the studio so I took my wife with me. For about five hours before filming we rehearsed. The drama went on and it was the scene in which a *shuriken* flew.

The moment that I positioned a *shuriken* and got ready to throw at the left sleeve of the woman standing in front of the sliding shutter, the actress screamed: "Wait! I cannot do it!" Mr Sasaki and the director talked over the matter but they could not change the scene. The actress was scared blue, something I well understood.

The time drew near and a strained feeling filled the studio. I made a proposal: "It is quite understandable that this lady who has just seen for the first time is afraid; but if you want to make this scene, isn't it possible to use a substitute actress?"

"Yes, but who? If no one else will do it, it amounts to the same thing."

Finally, I talked my wife into doing it. She too was scared, but at last made up her mind to do it. So presently, my wife appeared in the same kimono and wig as the actress, and there we were at the last rehearsal.

In the script , at the moment that the actress who was running away passed the sliding shutter, a *shuriken* flew at her from somewhere and fixed her right sleeve to the shutter. Immediately afterwards, the next *shuriken* fixed her sleeve so that she could not run away, and could be arrested...

I threw a blade, but it just fell down uselessly, because the sleeve was quite thick and because there was space between it and the shutter. I was in a jam. The time drew near relentlessly. The director and the other people in the studio were watching me and I felt that I was being driven into a corner.

As a last resort, we cut off the lining of the sleeve and let my wife stand nearer to the shutter. I threw and there was the sleeve fixed to the shutter. I was feeling relieved and prepared to act before the camera. The studio was crowded but quiet, they had started to film the first scene over in one corner. As I was wondering when my turn would come, the director pointed at me.

The real actress was running away, with the first camera trained on her. the second camera was taking my wife who was in the pose of running away in front of the sliding shutter. The director looked over with his eyes begging me. Abruptly, I found I could concentrate on hitting the centre of my wife's sleeve without a worry in my mind. "Ya!" The blade flew through the air, and struck the centre of the sleeve and fixed it to the flying shutter. I hadn't time to be pleased. "Got it!" I went around the camera to the right. I could feel at my back that all the members of the staff were watching me and holding their breath. As I was exclaiming, "Merciful Buddha! Once more!" with all my might, "*Butsuri*", the second blade was again stuck at the centre of the sleeve. The camera moved over and went on to the next scene.

At first I felt relieved but when I looked at the face of my wife, who was fixed to the sliding shutter, I noticed that her expression was petrified. Later she told me, "Your face was going from blue to white."

That was not a fight in earnest but it was beyond such a fight in some ways. When I face an enemy, even if I am to be beaten and die, I can accept it, realising my skills are imperfect. But in this case, if a blade was not stuck, a production which involved several hundred people would have broken down. When I think of my responsibility for it, even now, I can recall the strain I felt at the time. It was an unforgettable experience for me.

The reference date: 19th November, 1957. 20:30 to 21:00 JOKR T.V.
The title of the drama: "Doronko Hime"
A serial historical drama.
writer: Sasaki Ken
director: Tomie Shoji
Leading players: Matsushima Tomoko, Morikawa Shin, Tsuyuhara Chigusa.

34

THE FUNDAMENTAL THEME OF THE SHURIKEN ART

A LIVING BLADE

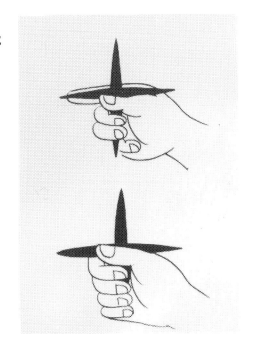

The art of *Shuriken* embodies a profoundly important way of life.

As I have mentioned before, there is an aspect of the *shuriken* art that has progressed from a military art and contains many elements that make our lives more enriched. The secrets of this invaluable way of life are the basis of all the arts and provide a code of living for many. The art of *shuriken* is, then, the priceless fruit left to us by our ancestors.

The most important point in the art of *shuriken* is how to hit the target correctly. In order to hit the target the blade needs to be especially balanced; this is not simply determined by the physical centre of gravity but depends on the ability of the artist and his method of throwing. Therefore, one blade will not be suitable for everybody and the only way of getting the ideal blade is to make it yourself. To do this it is necessary to file it down a little after each throw. this process usually has to be repeated several

A scene of throwing stones with a tool. *"Nenjyu Gyoji Inari Matsuri"*
The annual god, the fox god, of harvest festival. by Tosa Mitsunari.

hundred times or a thousand times before you have your own blade. This blade which is tailor made for your own hand and flies freely is called a 'living blade'. Sometimes it takes many days to make such a blade. The blade is then no longer simply a product of the artist's hands, but it is part of the body of the artist and contains his heart and soul. I often feel that 'this blade is living' or 'that blade contains life'.

HIRIU-KEN AND GINRIU-KEN

Although the shape of the blades is the same, each blade is different and it has individual characteristics just like human beings.

There are many different kinds of blades. There is one for short distances, one for long distances, one which is very light, one which is stiff, one which is sharp, and many others.

These individual characteristics are recognised intuitively as we grip the blades in our right hands preparing to throw them. When we recognise them we say "that blade!" the blades then have to be thrown to display their indvidual characters. Our former master made dozens of blades and tried to hit a target with them. He chose ten of them, and after a further trial chose five blades from the remaining ten. These five blades were used regularly, and gradually each blade showed itself to be of a superior or inferior quality. There were two that were exceptionally good at piercing the target and were named 'Hiriu-ken' and 'Ginriu-ken' – these were treated with great care.

He tried to make a replica of them. He was absorbed in making them the right size and weight and of the same kind of iron. But the state of striking, and the feeling he experienced as they left his hand were not the same. We learn about their individual characters according to the training given.

In your lifetime there are not many 'living blades' that will be just right for you only, and as you make progress the best blade for you will change.

A LIVING HIT AND A DEAD HIT

As I mentioned before there is a 'living blade'. Well, there is also a 'living hit'. Although we throw it under the control of our hand, according to the flying distance (*maai*) the blade sticks at the target as in figure A, at a further distance as in figure B, at yet a further distance as in figure C, and finally, at the farthest distance, it drops down without sticking as in figure D. (see page 88)

In the case where the blade which was thrown from a certain distance was stuck with the point of the blade higher than the tails in figure A, it means that it has the potential of being stuck from a farther distance, and we call it a 'living hit'. As we think about it, figure B looks like the most ideal hit; but in terms of *maai* (distance), it has reached its limit. If you throw it from even one step backward it sticks as in figure C. So although the hit of figure B is the zenith hit, there is no potential (power of life) in it. We call the hits of figures B as well as C,D, 'dead hit'. We always have to keep 'a live hit' in mind... To do this we should always refrain from using all of our strength at one time as it is important to remain one step away from perfection. This practice can be applied to your own lifetime, divided into three parts; A is youth, B will be manhood and C old age. In a sense you should live for the present and do your best without reaching perfection. In this way the art of throwing a *shuriken* has something in common with our own daily life.

THE ESSENCE OF KAMAE AND KATA

Concerning the *kamae* (postures) of *shuriken*, there are many different *kamae* according to the schools. I will now mention the *kamae* of '*Koso*' which is the fundamental *kamae* of the *Negishi-ryu*. As we can see from the picture of the *kamae* of *Koso*, there is a vertical line from the centre of the target to the ground. The big toe of the left foot is placed in front of the line whilst the big toe of the right foot is placed behind it. A few blades are held in the left hand and one blade at a time is taken by the right hand and positioned over the head. At this time the left and the right side of the blade, the navel, the larynx and the nose have to be on that line. To reach this position we twist half of the body at the waist and as the blade is thrown it is like a strong spring. At the moment when the work of the right arm, its wrist and the spring at the waist become one, you can throw the blade with a power beyond your imagination. But the left and right feet are on one line, it would be easy to lose your balance. At first we feel this method of throwing is too difficult and ask why we can't throw the blade more simply. We would like to throw it free style, but if we train and follow our instructors, finally we will discover that the traditional way of throwing is in fact the best.

From this fact we can establish that great importance was attached to the practice of '*kata*' in our traditional training, for example it is not only seen in the martial arts, but also in the *No* theatre, the tea ceremony and our music, because *kata* is the essence which our ancestors achieved after hard and long training.

Education begins by indoctrination of the essence; that is to say, strangely enough, that we start to teach from the conclusion. Here we can discover one essential element in Oriental education, namely schooling in the essence and continual training until one becomes practiced; that is, cultivation of the mind and comprehension until one achieves perfection.

From the point of view of modern education, it may be thought that this teaching method will remove the independent creative power of the individual. But, if the cultivation of the mind is complete and one's character reaches the limit of perfection, there will be gained the real creative power born in overcoming the final settlement of accounts of the past.

Couldn't we call this the real creative power which stands on the final settlement of accounts the past and remains aloof from it? And then the new '*kata*' will be created by this new power if we correctly adhere to the tradition. On the other hand, it should become something of the motive power creating the new power. '*Kaku*', which was spoken of by Basho, a Haiku poet, though dealing with a different field, really refers to this.

In '*So-o koketsu*', (The Oral Instruction of An Old Man) he mentioned the following:

If you don't obey *kaku* (the rule), you will go astray.

If you obey *kaku* (the rule), and you do not overcome it you will be narrow.

If you obey and overcome *kaku* (the rule), you will have good command of *kaku* (the rule).

In this case, I will apply *kaku* to the *Kata* of *shuriken*. It is most important to obey *kaku*, after pursuing the *kata* you will reach the state of being free and aloof.

In *shuriken* we start with formal training after which we at last acquire good command. In this manner *kata* or *Kamae* are to be taught.

KAMAE OF "KOKORO" (HEART OR MIND)

Kamae of "*koso*" is also a technique which is taught with the before mentioned training method. Concerning "*Koso*" in "*Densho*" (The Initiation), the frame of mind is taught as follows:

THE METHOD OF HOLDING A BLADE

The method of holding a blade differs according to the school and the distance, but there is a common factor; you must not exert excessive force in the palm and fingers when holding a blade. This principle applies not only in the martial arts but also in modern sports, for example, in golf and baseball.

The feeling when holding it in the hand must be like that of gently holding an egg. Do not put forth force nor grow stiff. Although your whole body is full of power "*Te no uchi*" the palm, should be soft and supple.

You tend to grip hard because you think if you do so with great force the blade flies powerfully farther. On the contrary, it is the reverse and the blade flys powerlessly. That is, it loses '*Ken no nobi*', the growth of the blade. '*Hanare*', the blade's departure from a hand must be very natural. It is ideal as if a bird slipped out of one's hand and took wing.

1. A cross shaped Hiraiken which was suggested by the cross shuriken of the Koga-ryu.

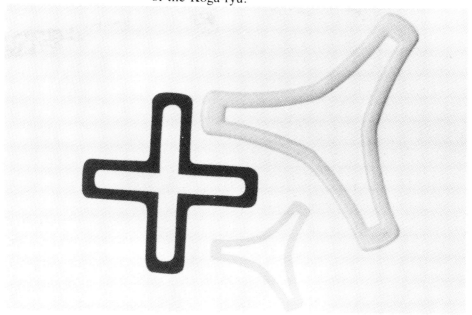

2. Fujigata Hiraiken. (Fuji shaped Hiraiken)

"Victory or defeat are not the result necessarily of good or bad skill. A brave man has no fear and is, therefore, pure and has no worldly thoughts. This wins a victory. Be aware of this. The *kamae* with "empty mind" is called "*Koso no I*".

The most important thing is to be empty minded, then you are able to achieve your best. Although *koso* is one of the *kamae* it must be performed naturally.

Miyamoto Musashi said in "*Gorin no sho*", Book of Five Rings.

"Whichever *kamae* it is, be ready to cut."

These words clearly illustrate the *kamae* of *Kōso*. On any occasion, we must be prepared to throw a blade at once. If I give it broader consideration, *kamae* is not merely the momentary posture when in possession of a blade; that is, our life itself is a continuation of *kamae*.

"Strategy is a frame of mind in our ordinary life – one's frame of mind is strategy." wrote Musashi.

41

'Nageru' to 'Utsu', Throw and strike.

The expression used for throwing a *shuriken* is 'strike', a distinction between throwing a *shuriken* and any other object. When throwing a blade, we must not throw it as we would a stone or a ball. When we cross swords and give a cut, the point of the sword cuts as we try to pierce the middle of the forehead of a foe through with a shout... Our instructor said that we must make the blade strike with this feeling. We say *'Uchit-sukeru'*, strike, as a word which exactly illustrates this spirit. Therefore the *shuriken* is not a sneaking missile which we throw from a safe and unseen place.

In some ways, *shuriken* is used to explain the ways of the swordsmanship. For example, in *'Honshiki Mondo'* which teaches the swordsmanship of the *Yagyu* School another school teaches *shuriken*. *Shuriken* is a blade approximately 10cm in length and thrown turning it in the palm. Although we do not throw a *tachi* or spear the way of handling them is exactly the same. Why should we differentiate between these arts.

Now returning to our subject. How does it strike and fly through the air? I have already described how to hold a blade, and blades which are struck in many ways reach a target in various ways of flying; roughly *choku-da*, the direct hit (strike), *Ikkaiten-da*, the one turn hit, and *takaiten-da*, the multi-turn hit.

In consequence of their efforts, our ancestors invented a distinctive and unique blade. This coincided with the theory of aerodynamics. That is, by fixing a distinctive tail at the end of the blade, air resistance would be set up which would control the turning of the blade.

The Way of Throwing – Direct-Strike Method

In the first direct strike method, we hold the point of the blade towards the target and merely strike it. This will be assumed to be the easiest but, in fact, as you will discover if you try it, the blade turns and does not fly in a straight line. In order to achieve a straight strike, at the moment the blade leaves the hand, turning must be controlled by the knack of 'snap', a technique used in baseball. That is, at the last moment, when the tail of the blade goes through the hand, moderate pressure is put on the tail with the inside of the forefinger. As representative schools of this method, there are the *Kato-no*, *Negishi* and *Shindo-ryu* which I have mentioned previously. Although we control the turning in the air, the effective strike has a limited distance of approximately 5.5m.

In view of this, in the *Katori-Shinto-Ryu*, a blade is thrown between foes within this distance. It is a distinction of the *ryu* to throw from a fixed distance with the fixed shape blade. Isn't there any way to overcome this limit of distance? Yes, the *Negishi-ryu* invented a new method of controlling turning which overcame the limit of hand-control.

The One-turn Strike Method

In this case, a blade is thrown and once in the air before it reaches the target. It is held with the point facing the thrower and the tail facing the target. *Shirai-ryu* is the representative school of this method of hitting. The shape of the blade in this school is like that of a tongue and the most simple. The method of holding it varies according to the distance thrown without any change in the blade itself or its shape. This is also one of the secrets. For short distances, the tail of the blade should be a little forward and, for long distances, it should be a little more forward. By this method, the air speed of the blade is controlled and it hits the target at the most effective angle.

The Multi-turn Strike Method

Once a blade is thrown, it turns in flight according to the law of nature. Figure No.1 shows one of the incorrect ways of holding a *shuriken*. If one holds it in this manner it usually strikes the target at too low a position and the rate of successful hits are few: therefore you should hold it like figure No. 2, 3. It is the natural way to throw a blade. The blades are cross shaped or eight pointed in order to stick in the target at any point no matter who throws it. But, if it is aimed to hit a target correctly, it is quite difficult. To hold the blade, the forefinger must be stretched in order to point at the target and the other three fingers must grip the blade firmly.

This method of throwing is the easiest but has many faults such as slow speed, noise and shallow sticking due to great air resistance. These should not be used as weapons.

Let us now consider these three methods.

In the direct hit method, we try to overcome the natural tendency to turn by training ourselves and by applying physical theory (devising of the tail).

The one-turn hit is achieved by acknowledging and following the natural law but limiting this to one turn only, thus condensing the power of nature.

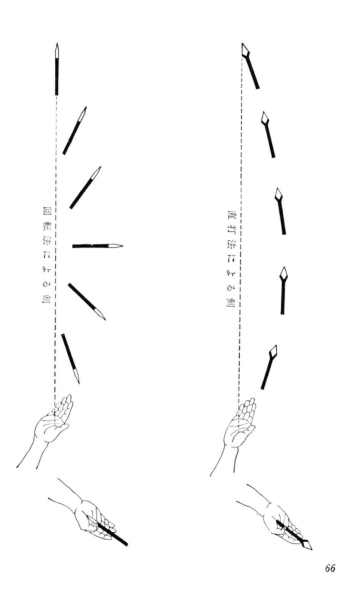

1. The flying state of a direct hit.
2. The flying state of a turning hit.

The multi-turn hit is achieved by following the natural law and adapting oneself to it.

It is very interesting to see the shapes which were manifested from many formulas as a result of human thought on the subject of nature, the method of dealing with nature and the individual character, even in the technique in which one just throws a blade although the meaning has now been lost. Next, I shall tell you about '*Maai*' which is one of the most important teachings in the martial arts from the *shuriken's* point of view.

Maai – Distance of Stillness

I have often used this expression before; it means the *maai,* or distance between oneself and a target or foe. The maximum interval in *shuriken* is one half of the interval in archery; that is, approximately 13.6m. A throw of greater distance falls into the category of archery. But the effective distance in *Shuriken* is actually between 5m and 9m.

Initial training consists of hitting the target at a distance of only one pace but gradually, step by step, the distance is increased. 'We wish to hit the target from one step further away' is, of course, the greatest wish of beginners. In a gradual process, one eventually reaches a distance from which it is impossible to hit the target. This distance depends on the individual but is usually about 3.5m to 4.5m. Here, the *shuriken* trainee worries about getting over the barrier but, after the effort of 'three years for one step' is continued, this problem is gradually solved.

The Distance of Movement

Can we make strike with a blade from any distance after we get over the wall of 'three years for one step'? The answer is 'No'. After that there is a problem for every step. The only difference between us and a beginner is that we are aware and gaining a strong power of resistance to difficulty and we can push the training straight forward. Within, we may take up the distance to 7 or 8m, but we come to a new wall again. We have a Master who sees this, and initiates instruction at the correct time, "a degree of strength and weakness". The greater distance the greater the action; we have to put in the power appropriate for every action, and in this case the power must be even.

During my time as a beginner, I saw my master hit a blade from a long distance, and I wondered why he didn't use more power. It looked like a powerless way of hitting, but it flew a long distance and was obviously a strong hit. He had completely learned the "*Kyō-Jaku no do*", a degree of strength and weakness. First we learn thoroughly the posture for the interval and the handling of a blade in the hand. After that, we strain to be able to hit a blade in conformity with the distance. We then try various blades. Eventually, we can stick a blade in a target from any distance, and this is when we have overcome "*Dō No Maai*", the Distance of Movement.

But when we really face a foe, the distance becomes much more complicated because as we move, so will the foe. We do not throw a blade at the foe at the present distance, but at the next moment, in the future distance. After we have completed the above described training, we train to strike blades at targets as we run. It is very similar to *Yabusame* in archery. The training of "*Sei No Maai*", Still distance, has laid the groundwork for "*Dō No Maai*", the Distance of Movement.

AIM

It is a fundamental rule that we take aim with the whole of our body. If we strike with a blade in the correct posture, the blade flies correctly to the target. If the right and the left hands hold blades, the throat, the nose, the head must be all in the one line which would be drawn from the target and the blade in the right hand is thrown out using a twist of the waist. The blade will fly on this line.

We are strictly told: "Never take aim with your eyes", because by taking aim with our eyes we naturally strike with a blade with the finger tips and deviate from a fundamental rule. Only the correct *kamae* of the body allows us to hit the target. It is the same in archery as we really correctly define our body being satisfactorily "bending a bow to the full" and coming to the "moment", the target grows bigger and comes toward you, you seem to at last enter the target, and you never miss the aim. Our ancestors said this, "Take aim with the navel". It does not seem to make sense, but when you try it, you know it is very natural.

The word of *Zen* by the Zen priest Dogen in *Shōbogenzō* said: "We don't testify our own way but the Way lets us testify". I think this coincides with the idea of taking aim at a target. When we take aim strenuously, the target seems to get smaller and smaller and seems to be moving away. We should not only take aim at the target, we should

46

stand toward the target and concentrate our whole mind and will upon achieving the right posture; then we can gain real aim and a correct hit.

As part of training, it is good to learn not to aim with the fingers by throwing with closing our eyes or blind-folded. Also, the action of aim lets us strike truly as our mind is only "*mu*" (nothing) (Shin-no-Atari).

Our master told us the following story of his experience: "I was at a loss, and late one night I called on my old master Tonegawa. After he had listened to my story in silence, he quietly stood up and took me to a pitch dark *Dojo*. As he stood in the centre of the dark *Dojo*, he quietly raised a blade over his head and hit the first blade into pitch dark space with a piercing shout. The next sound was the blade piercing a thick target through: "*Gatsu*". On the heels of the first blade followed a second and in a moment my ears were struck by a thick, unusual sound. "Naruse, go and look at the target". When I approached the target, I found a wonderful thing. The first blade had pierced through the very centre of the target, the second one had stuck in the wooden tail of the first. I was moved by an inexpressibly sublime feeling, and vacantly stood in the darkness for sometime, forgetting to draw the blade".

The old master had shown his student "the true aim of no aim".

QUICK HIT AND THE TIME

The first blade is held in the right hand and other blades are held in the left hand. As soon as the first blade has left the hand you must prepare to hit the second blade in case the foe has moved and a second blade is necessary. We usually say, "five blades in one breath", and have been trained to throw five blades in one breath; but keeping time with the foe is the problem. Musashi mentioned in "*Gorin-no-sho*": "In the way of military accomplishments, shooting an arrow and shooting a gun, even to riding a horse, there are time and rhythm.

When we spring a blade from "the time of '*Ku*' " (emptiness) there is a way to overcome physical time. Musashi also wrote: "Quickness in tactics is not the real way as quickness does not coincide with the interval of the time, so you should know that quickness is late". Again he said: "Quickness is especially bad in the way of tactics". Here, he is strongly warning us not to be enslaved to the quickness of time. But in order to come into the world of time, overcoming the time, we need to train thoroughly to the limit of the quickness of time. Otherwise, we cannot overcome the world of "real quickness."

IN-YO-SO (THE STRUGGLE OF YIN-YANG)

As I mentioned before, hold a blade with the right hand over the head, the next blade in the left hand and take a posture against a foe. We call this posture '*Kōsō- No-I*'. With this posture first of all, we strike with the first blade, the second and the third, one after another, before a foe takes a posture. This strategy is called '*In-Yō-Sō*' (the fight of male and female principles) in the *Shuriken* art. This is one of the original concepts of Oriental philosophy and, we could say, of the oriental universal view. We divide all things in the universe into the two elements '*in*' and '*yo*', and all growth and prosperity is the result of the interaction of these elements.

In the *Shuriken* art we think of '*Kōsō-No-I*' as '*yo*' because it is a posture full of energy for hitting a blade. At the moment that we hit the blade in the right hand and all the energy comes out, we understand that it changes from '*yo*' to '*in*', and when the blade reaches the foe, we think '*in*' has reached the limit. We say of the moment we used up all of the energy that "*In Ni Ochita*", '*yo*' has fallen into '*in*'. The mind and body is in '*Kyo*', the unprepared, unguarded state. If we beat the foe with the first blade, it is good. But if we don't beat the foe and he receives it and begins to attack us while we are still unprepared, he is in the state of '*yo*' or '*Jitsu*' and we are defeated in strategy and the martial art. The states of '*Jitsu*' and '*kyo*' are one of the most important elements in orientalism, especially the 'thought of strategists' which is discussed by the Chinese strategist Sonshi (Sun Tzu). He said: "You should not willingly stand on the defensive because a foe may catch you napping, off your guard." An attack comes from the limits of '*yo*' and is fought out in the current and energy that change it to '*in*'. We must not stay there but must soon change back to '*yo*' to attack again. We express the change from '*yo*' to '*in*' to '*yo*' as '*In-Yo– Sō*', the 'Fight of *In* and *Yo* (Yin and Yang).

Jōseishi stated: "Recently the days have become longer and in May there is much liveliness at 3.00 p.m., but because of their very length, they will gradually get shorter." In the beginning, '*in*' is not brilliant, but it is the beginning of what is going to be great at the end. As technique, we *kamae* in '*yo*', strike with the blade before the foe is ready, and rapidly strike with the second and the third. We do not remain in '*in*', nor do we stay at the limit of '*yo*', but we strike with blades one after the other and attack. This corresponds to the theory of growth and prosperity based on the dualism of the male and female principles of the Oriental view of the universe that I mentioned before. In 'the *denshō*' (licence of the *ryū* in *Kobudo*) it is concisely stated: "About the fight of *In-Yo*, we kamae and it becomes '*yo*' and we hit and it turns to '*in*', again we *kamae* and it becomes '*yo*' etc. There is not any gap between the undulation of '*in*' and '*yo*'. The poles are on a straight way."

RECEIVING A BLADE

As we train to throw a blade at a target, we also learn to receive a blade thrown by a foe. If we do not learn them both it means that we are only training in the '*Sei-no-maai*', 'Distance of Stillness', without training in the 'Distance of Movement', and we would not call this the true living martial art.

I remember the old story of Mori Gentatsu. In order to complete his grasp of the art, he made up his mind to challenge Yagyu Jubei who was the best swordsman of the time, to a match. In the first match, Jubei used a *bokken*, or wooden sword, and Gentatsu used *shurikens* in their cases, and three of the *shurikens* hit the body of Jubei. In the second game, Jubei asked Gentatsu to use real blades, and facing him with a *tessen*, or iron fan, struck down all of the blades.

It can easily be sensed that Jubei had great experience at this game, for an important part of the secret book of his school expressed the characters of *shuriken* with special meaning, and training in receiving the *shuriken* is particularly emphasised. For example, in one sentence of *Yagyu 'Yagyu-ryu Shinhiden-sho'* it says: "It is too late to act after we see a blade flying through the air. While the *shuriken* is still in the hand of the foe, we have to anticipate the projection of the throw and plan our movement in tune with it to cut it down." If not, we cannot cut his blades down when they reach our sphere of action. You will wonder why we can cut them down when they haven't yet come, but this is an expression often used and understood. For example, in *Iai-jutsu*, we have cut an opponent before we draw out a sword and we have to understand that we have already killed him. It is one example showing how we are taught. "*Iai* is in the scabbard."

THE PLIANT MIND (MUSASHI AND DOGEN)

When throwing a *shuriken*, the most important thing is to remember that for a good strike all of your muscles, your wrist, and your mind should be in a 'soft' or 'free' state.

We can strike at a target strongly and correctly when both mind and body are soft, but when you lose the softness, that is, in case of need, the blade has died. Not only in *shuriken*, but in any art, 'softness' is needed to produce the highest ability. As we grow stiff, the turning of the blade in the air quickens. Even if we intend to throw a blade at a 7m interval it becomes the best angle in the neighborhood of 5.5m; as it reaches a target of 7m over the 5,5m which is the boundary between a living hit and a dead hit, the turning angle has already passed and the blade becomes a 'dead blade'. It has completely lost the power to give a foe a hit. In order not to grow stiff, it is necessary to train our minds as well as daily practising our technique.

In '*Kencho*', Heizan Shiryu says: "I have never heard that an expert in sword and spear or someone who is said to be a master, had rendered distinguished service at the battle field. An expert in shooting, Inatomi Ichimu, could shoot a willow leaf at 100 steps away and even he guessed the location of a bird on the roof from its singing as he was in a thatched house and shot it down. But this expert could not shoot a single foe at the Korean war."

We cannot gain softness in a day. But if we train mind and body steadily, we will eventually gain it. Miyamoto Musashi said: "As we master the way of the sword, the whole body and the mind become soft; we learn the rhythm, the body and the legs become loose at will and we can defeat one after the other. We gradually learn the right from the wrong tactics." I think of this in terms of *Zen*. When *Zen* master Dogen had finished a long period studying *Zen* in China he returned home and said: I came back with nothing but a pliant mind." As I throw my blade, I often reflect on this.

SHURIKEN IN THE CINEMA

There was a scene portraying the throwing of a kitchen knife in the film '*Tsubaki Sanjuro*' which was directed by Mifuni Toshiro. I suppose he threw it by direct hit, but it wouldn't have stuck from a long distance. I was not sure of the distance because it was a film, but as I watched I was thinking that he should have thrown it from one step forward. There was also an expert in throwing knives in the film '*The Magnificent Seven*' played by James Coburn. I think it would be impossible to throw a knife from a great distance, but he managed the throw of '*Uranami*' (under throw) very well. In the film '*Gunfight at the OK Corral*', the character Doc Holliday threw a hidden knife from his boot at the last moment and surprised his foe. We call this '*In-ken*' and it is considered to be a secret thing. It is said that the unorthodox style of Araki Mataemon was to put a few blades into his head band, throwing them at the right moment to rescue his allies; but I dare say that he never really did anything like that because it would let a foe know how many blades he had which is thought to be an unskilled thing to do. However, if he had thrown all of the blades in the head band, he would relax, and could be attacked by surprise with the hidden blade. Actually, throwing a blade from the head band is very quick because we omit the act of bringing it up.

THE THROWING COIN OF ZENIGATA HEIJI

In '*Zinigata Heiji Torimono-Cho*' by Nomura Kodo, every time he was in trouble, Heiji, the main character, took a coin from his bosom at the critical moment, and rapidly throwing it at the villains, defeated them. This scene, which occurred several times, always left me feeling refreshed.

I suppose that the author got the idea from the throwing art of '*Hishi Gane*' (lozenge – coin) which was often used by Ninja of Iga or Koga in the Tokugawa period. This *hishi gane* was a lozenge shaped coin, about 6cm in length, 5cm in width, and 0.3cm in thickness with a hole in the centre. He put a rope through the hole and carried it with him always, throwing it when it was needed. In the book, the author changed it to a round shape and it became a 'throwing coin' as Heiji's speciality. There are no details in the book about how he held or threw it, but I think if you wanted to hit a target you should throw lengthwise as you throw the cross *shuriken*. The film 'Heiji Oyabun',*Boss Heiji*, starring Hasegawa Kazuo or Ōkawa Hashizo, showed him throwing it with a 'sidearm throw'; but from my experience, it would be hard to hit a target that way.

1. Hishi gata (a lozenge shaped coin)
2. A variation

菱形（上）とその変形（下）

51

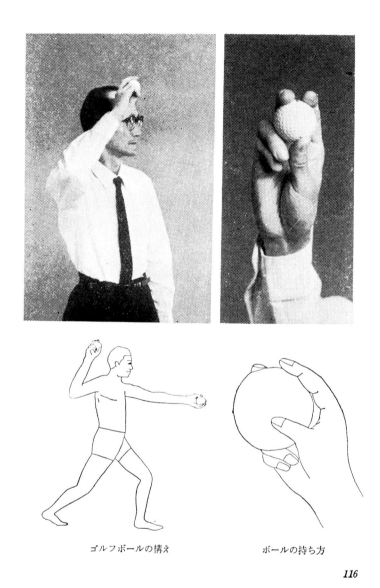

ゴルフボールの構え　　　　　　　ボールの持ち方

1. The Kamae with a golf ball.
2. The way of holding a golf ball.

THE ART OF SELF DEFENCE WITH A GOLF BALL

The *shuriken* is the smallest weapon that can be taken with us anywhere, but it is very dangerous and can lead to trouble because we are trained to attack a foe with a fatal blow, and even in the cause of justice, we do not want to cause so much harm. So I now recommend the technique of self defence with a golf ball instead of a *shuriken*, using the training of throwing a *shuriken*. If someone who has finished the foundation training of throwing throws a golf ball, he can display astonishing power. This is a very useful self-defence weapon for women who must walk alone at night for they can simply carry a few balls in their handbags. The technique is similar to '*Hayauchi*' (the quick hit) in *shuriken*. We use two balls, the second ball is held in the left hand and we get ready to throw it as soon as the first ball is thrown. (Hold a ball as in Figure 1 and throw it as in Figure 2).

BASEBALL AND SHURIKEN

There is a relationship between modern baseball and the *shuriken*. It is very interesting to watch the batting form of *Kondo Kazuhiko* and *Sadaji* (who are well known as the 'Kings of the *Yomiuri* Giants') from the point of view of the *shuriken* art.

First of all, when *Kondo* stands at the batting box, he moves the bat as if drawing an elliptical locus according to the wind-up of the pitcher. As I watched this I thought of a scene which *Miyamote Musashi* fought with *Shishido Baiken* of *Iga Ueno*, who was an expert in *Kusarigama-jutsu* (a technique employing a sickle and chain weapon). *Musashi* was an expert in dagger throwing, and in fighting with two swords.

At the fight, *Baiken* was turning a *fundo* (made of iron or brass, oval, square or hexagon shaped)) over his head like a windmill and positioning a sickle low in the left hand. He was attacking *Musashi* who positioned a *wakizashi* (dagger) in his right hand over his head. At the moment that the sound of the turning of the dagger and sound of the turning of the *fundo* became one tune, the *fundo* of *Baiken* flew to the face of *Musashi* but, one moment quicker, the dagger of *Musashi* left his right hand and pierced the chest of *Baiken*.

Aibyoshi (timing with the other)

The word for the turning of the dagger of *Musashi* is '*Aibyoshi*'. We can say that the turning of the bat of *Kondo* is also 'in time with' the motion of the pitcher. As to a moment before batting, he lifts his right leg and stands on one leg; this means that by this motion not only he transfers the centre of gravity but also he adjusts himself to be in time with the pitcher. Both have a high batting average this way. But *Musashi* said late in his life that it is a desirable stage to pass to this exaggerated stage of being in time with the other as soon as we can.

In the training process of *shuriken*, we move either our foot position or the point of a blade according to the adversary's or opponent's motion, but it is not good to make this obvious. If a pitcher momentarily avoids the time of the batter and throws the ball while the batter's motion is too much 'in time with the other', it will have become a fault.

In the field of victory or defeat in the Martial Arts, the main point is to take the time of the other, or to avoid the time of the other and attack. *Musashi* wrote in '*Gorin-no-sho*': 'Everything has timing, and especially in training it is necessary to use timing in tactics. It is a principle of tactics that first we must learn about time, discerning the different moments, choosing the correct moment among many, knowing the time of the interval and the time to attack. In a fight of tactics, know the opponent's timing and beat him with a timing he cannot achieve, and with no substantial time'. If they listen to the words of the sword saint, *Musashi*, the possibilities in the field of baseball will be enhanced. A pitcher will let his batter take his time, and at the moment that batter has completely fallen into his own rhythm, will avoid that rhythm and throw his ball in another. And I hope that a pitcher will appear who can throw a ball without any batter spotting his timing. On the other hand, a batter who can learn the timing of the pitcher and not show any emotion and can conform to any time will be known as a great batter. In this view, if the point of the bat of *Kondo* does not move an inch, and his legs are on the ground like a rock, the pitcher will be uneasy, and if they think out the time in secret, their batting average will be improved. This is how the *shuriken* art can be applied to baseball.

In the *shuriken* art, when facing a foe, there is a teaching: 'Absorb up the whole time of the movement of the foe into the forefinger of the left hand'. After this, I would like to advise both of them to learn the movement of the pitcher by stretching the point

of the first joint of the right hand instead of the movement of lifting the leg. Someone who improves from his own motion of '*Aibyoshi*' (timing out or in with the other) to the extension and contraction of his finger can then just forget about the finger and just hit the various balls with ease, at last coming into the free state that marks the real batter. This is in common with the state of the *Itto Musoken-ryu* which is sung in a poem: '*Tsukuba Yama, Hayama, Hansan shigekeredo. Uchikomu Tach-wa shin no itto*'. (Mount Tsukibo is covered with leaves
Yet, there is only one sword to strike with).

ICHIRYU ITTŌ AND THE SHURIKEN

There is a story about a shuriken expert, Ichiryu Ittō, in a book called 'Great Swordsmen – Fact and Fiction' by Watatana-Kyoshi (his pen name – Tobushi Tahei). This is based on the 8th volume of '*Sekisui Zatsuwa*' and written to be a true record. It is quite a long story but as the information imparts the spirit of *shuriken* and its artistry I shall quote it.

'There was a naughty boy who worked for Mizuno Kenmotsu Tadayoshi in Sanshu Okazaki as a cleaner. He was about fifteen years old. One day he went out to the veranda of the study in Okazaki castle and saw a worm hole by the bamboo gutter. He was so bored that anything served as a diversion. He tore a sheet of tissue paper, put it into his mouth and chewed it to make a ball. He picked it up with his finger tips and threw it lightly at the worm hole. The paper pellet missed the hole and stuck near it. He was not satisfied, and he did it once more. This time the paper pellet was much nearer the hole.

"Once more!" he said to himself and again he chewed the paper noisily and threw it, and sometimes he could hit the hole which encouraged him. He continued like this for one or two hours. The next day as soon as he had finished cleaning, he came to the same place and spent his time in the same way. The eaves became white, covered with paper pellets stuck like birds droppings.

"My goodness, I shall be scolded." he thought. So he changed the paper pellets to beans. Wonderful! According to the amount of practice the percentage hits got better. At first he could only hit the target once out of thirty or forty times, but after ten days he succeeded in hitting two or three times out of ten, although after this he could not make visible progress. However, after contiuous practice for half a year, he did not miss once.

"Good! I shall make my way in the world as a master of the martial arts, it is no use being a cleaning boy forever," he thought. As soon as he made up his mind, he devoted himself to practice until he was able to hit the target from 15m with a real *shuriken* of 6cm in length.

He knew that the *shuriken* art was not considered important enough to make for him his way in the world, so he took up the martial arts which were essential if he wanted to become *samurai*. He overcame hardship, in his formidable zeal to become a master of the martial arts and eventually he obtained a license. His secret skill in *shuriken* was exquisite, he could even hit a fly about 2m by throwing a sewing needle.

He left the Mizunos and went to Edo to open a *dojo* with nis new name, Ichiryu Ittō. Later he was employed by a clan in the Tōhoku Area and attended the lord's mansion in Edo. At last his dream came true, but a great difficulty awaited him.

One of his colleagues exchanged Ittō's sword for his by mistake. To his surprise it was too light. When he drew out the sword it was a bamboo blade. He realized that is was Ichiryu Ittō's, so he went to exchange it for his own sword. He said to Ichiryu's manservant jokingly:

"If this sword is anything to go by your master's short sword must be bamboo too."

"Yes sir, my master's *dai-sho*, a pair of swords, are only for show – the blades are made of wood," the manservant replied. The rumour spread throughout the Edo mansion and finally reached the lord. The lord ordered,

"A traitor! A thief! Catch him swiftly and excute him!"

As a warning to others, it was not good enough merely to execute him. First of all one of the skilful attendants was chosen to perform the command of the lord. They summoned Ittō to subdue the attendant who pretended to be mad and shut himself up in a room, with a sword drawn, but at the same time in the room the attendant lay in wait to kill Ichiryu when he entered.

Ichiryu was led to the front of the room by a senior *samurai*.

"It is the room, be on your guard." the *samurai* said.

"Yes sir." Ichiryu Ittō took off his *kimono*, and the bamboo *dai-sho*, then put them by his feet.

"I say! You are not going into the room without your sword, are you? The madman has sword," the *samurai* said.

"No, It will be all right! I shall cut him down soon, so please be a witness." Ittō replied. He drew open the door. There waiting for Ittō ready to cut him down was the attendant with his sword drawn.

Ittō advanced and stopped 9 m in front of him.

"You offended the will of your lord and shut yourself in the room ignoring your offence. I will execute you by the command of the lord," he declared.

"Be quiet, if you come closer I'll kill you," the attendant said.

"I'll not come near you. Be prepared!" At that moment he took out two *shuriken* from his *kimono* and stepped one foot forward.

"Eiya!" He swung his hand with a yell. The two *shuriken* drew two lines in the air and pierced the man's eyes, and his opponent fell over. Ichiryu then made a dash at him, picked up the man's sword and cut off his head.

"Sir, I successfully killed him," said Ittō. He bowed to the samurai and strode out of the room, and then ran away from Edo. He saw through the plot of the execution commanded by the lord.

"It is absurd to serve such a careless clan as this," he murmured. Later he found relief in the Satake family of the Akitsu clan and his salary was doubled...'

It is a pity we do not know what shape of blade Ichiryu Ittō used, but the phrase "After practising for half a year..." explains the difficulty of learning the *shuriken* art properly. "He trained himself to hit a target from 12m..." or "Ittō stopped at 9m this side of the enemy..." The former phrases tell us '*maai*', the distance. The fact that he pierced through both eyes accurately describes the *shuriken* art. The most important part is that his *dai-sho* were made of bamboo. There was not any explanation why he had to wear them. I do not think that this means he neglected the spirit of the *bushi*; on the contrary, it is very typical of the master of the *shuriken* art. This is, they believed in the blade of 9cm and in the success of fighting with it.

The expert in the *shuriken* art, Katono Izu of the Sendai clan, was said to be wearing *shuriken* in his hair and did not carry any *dai-sho* in his later years. The two stories have much in common.

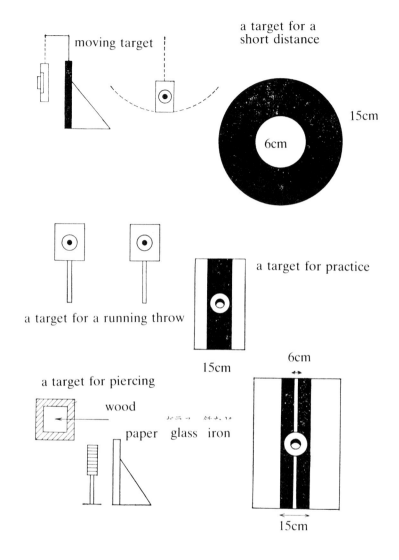

moving target

a target for a
short distance

15cm

6cm

a target for practice

a target for a running throw

15cm

6cm

a target for piercing

wood

paper   glass   iron

15cm

various targets

58

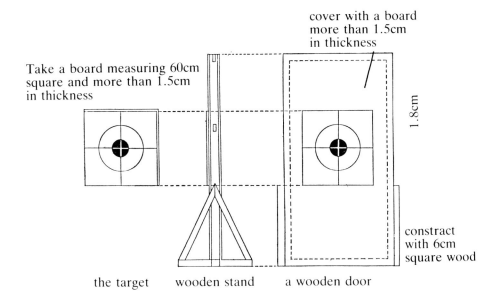

Take a board measuring 60cm square and more than 1.5cm in thickness

cover with a board more than 1.5cm in thickness

1.8cm

constract with 6cm square wood

the target   wooden stand   a wooden door

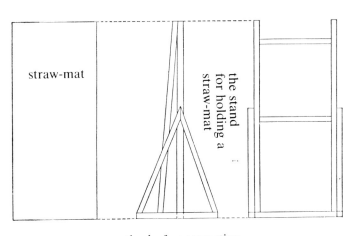

straw-mat

the stand for holding a straw-mat

method of construction

59

THE TARGET

A *shuriken* target is made of a wooden board, more than 1.5cm in thickness, or a straw-mat covered with target paper. If the board is thin a blade bounces back. It is preferable to use a soft and thick board. In the case of training a straw-mat is better, so as not to damage the blade.

As to the standard size of the target it consists of an outer circle, 35cm accross and has an inner circle (a black mark), 9.5cm across.

Its height should be above the knee of the person who throws.

I used to use a target with an outer circle 15cm across and the inner circle 9cm across. The outer circle should be roughly the same size as my face, and the distance between both my pupils for the inner circle.

A wooden target gives a better feeling of the moment when the blade strikes and for the training of penetration.

The stand and setting of the target is as in the illustration.

Men of old struck at a tree in high mountains and secluded valleys.

Through my experience I am convinced that it is necessary to strike a hard board, but it is more useful to pierce the paper in a wooden frame and aim not to tear a paper for the practice session. The latter is most difficult. That is, if the blade slants slightly it will make a large hole after piercing it. If there is a person who is able to pierce the paper without making a hole larger than the blade, he is a real master.

To practice 'Dō no Maai', the distance of movement, as before mentioned, set up many targets at intervals, strike them one after another, as you run like that of *Yabusame* archery.

And, as in the illustration, hang a moving target like a pendulum and strike it.

However, these practices should be done after one has mastered the basic training as I mention in the following chapter.

Draw a vertical line on the target for the practice session and try to strike the line, you will make good progress. The fact that the blade misses the line means the basic posture is out of balance.

甲賀流・伊賀流十字手裏剣　　四方手裏剣　　甲賀流・伊賀流手裏剣　　甲賀流・伊賀流八方手裏剣

小堀流万字手裏剣　　小堀流手裏剣　　柳生流十字手裏剣　　狐伝流・諸賞流手裏剣
（車剣，糸巻剣ともいう）

五方手裏剣　　柳生流・甲賀流十字手裏剣　　四方手裏剣　　三光手裏剣
（星状手裏剣）

1. Koga-ryu, Iga-ryu Jyuji (cross) shuriken
2. Shihō shuriken (pointed out in four directions)
3. Koga-ryu, Iga-ryu shuriken
4. Koga-ryu, Iga-ryu Happō shuriken (pointed out in eight
directions)
5. Kobori-ryu Manji shuriken (swastika shape)
6. Kobori-ryu shuriken
7. Yagyu-ryu Jyuji shuriken (cross)
8. Koden-ryu, Shoshō-ryu shuriken. Sha-ken or wheel shaped.
Itomaki-ken (bobbin shaped)
9. Gohō shuriken (pointed out in five directions)
or Hoshijō shuriken (star shaped)
10. Yagyu-ryu, Koga-ryu Jyuji shuriken (a cross shaped)
11. Shilhō shuriken. (pointed out in four directions)
12. Shankō shuriken

74

THE BASIC FORM OF SHURIKEN ART

MANJI-NO-KATA

As I mentioned before, there are many schools in *shuriken*, but I will write out the basic form common to all the schools. The form is called *Manji* (swastika) form, *Metsuke* (deciding a position and looking at the target), *Karade-Sabaki* (handling of one's body), *Tenouchi* (in hand), and *Zanshin* (alertness of the mind after throwing the *shuriken*), which are the most important things to throwing the *shuriken*.

NYŪJŌ (ENTRANCE)

When entering before the performance of the Martial Arts, we salute the *Gosaishin*, the enshrined deity, and holding a *shuriken* in the right hand, step quietly towards the target with the handle, that is, the tail parts of the *shuriken* towards the target. When we reach the planned distance (about 4cm or 9cm) we stop and make a bow to the target.

METSUKE

We decide the right position by seeing where the centre of the target coincides with the position of our own navel and vertically drop the line onto the floor from the centre of the target, then extend the line to oneself, and as we are putting our centre on the line look hard at the target. We call this *metsuke*, but we do not call it *metsuke* if the target is aimed only with the eyes.

ASHIGAMAE

After saluting the target, we stand naturally on the imaginary line, then closing our feet from the natural position, step on the line with the big toe of one foot and then drawing the right foot along the line as well, step on the line with the big toe.

PASSING A SHURIKEN FROM ONE HAND TO THE OTHER

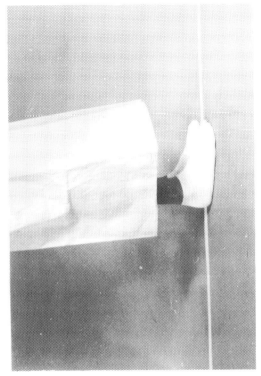

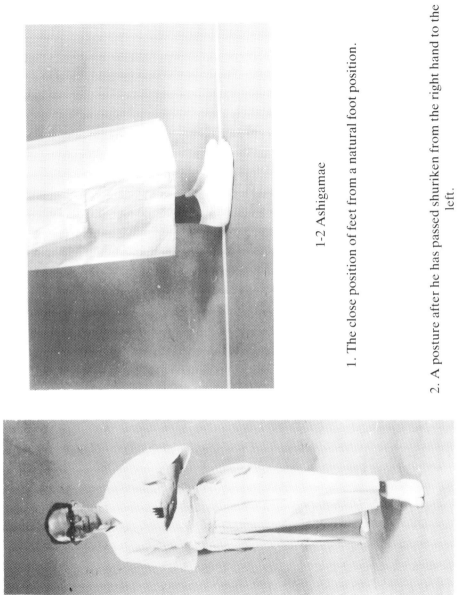

1-2 Ashigamae

1. The close position of feet from a natural foot position.

2. A posture after he has passed shuriken from the right hand to the left.

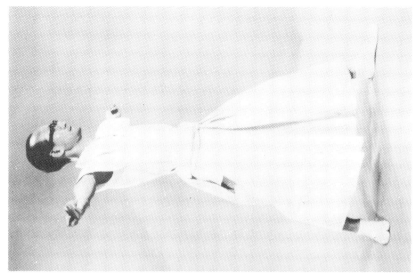

1. The first movement from the front.

2. The first movement from the side.

64

3. Shuriken no kamae.

Move it to the left hand with the forefinger extended along the *shuriken* pointing forward. During this act it is important that we should not take our eyes off the target.

POSTURE OF THE BODY

As we have moved a *shuriken* from the right hand to the left hand, lower the right hand quietly, continually lowering the left hand with the *shuriken*, gathering power in the abdomen without bending forward or backward, that is '*Furitsu-Fukutsu*', '*no standing and no bending*' *posture.*

THE WAY OF TAKING A BLADE AND HOLDING A BLADE

Carefully taking the blade with the right hand from the blades held in the left hand and looking hard at the target as if an eagle is just going to open its wings, get ready.

THE FIRST MOVEMENT

Take a blade, raise both hands straight to the right and the left, take a firm step, balance the body slightly upright, stretch both hands out and look hard at the target.

THE SECOND MOVEMENT

Turn the left hand foward a quarter and the right hand backward a quarter letting the body agree with the line as if the body was twisted from the left to the right. In this case the body should agree exactly with the line. Next, *kamae* (position) a blade in the right hand above the right back of the head, and aim the point of the blade in the left hand at the target. We call this is '*Shuriken-no-kane*'.

THE THIRD MOVEMENT

At last we throw the blade as if a twisted strength is unleashed, hitting straight by its irresistible vitality. We don't throw with an open hand, but as if a captured bird flies away through the hand, or at the moment we drew a dagger and strike, the point flies off to its target.

66

ZANSHIN

When a blade has struck at a target, the right hand, which threw the blade, is raised up over the forehead as if in reaction to the throw; and one should look hard at the target in this posture. We call this 'zanshin' which doesn't mean a still posture. In a fighting situation, we now have to move to the next movement (drawing a sword to cut into the foe or throwing a second *shuriken*).

THE END

After we have thrown a blade, we put back the right foot forward, open to a natural position and at the same time put the hands back into the first posture and the end the performance of the martial art.

EXIT

After saluting the target, step back towards the exit, stop at a suitable place, salute the *Gosaishin* (the enshrined deity) and leave the area.

That is the outline of the 'Manji-no-kata', this form is the most important movement in making up the basic posture in *shuriken*; it is necessary to practice this again and again. The movement of this form is three times, but we can omit the part of raising the right hand and the left hand, then *kamae* the left hand forward and take a blade with the right hand and *kamae*. This is the double movement and we call it '*tōji*'. The single movement is called '*chokushi*'.

THE FORM OF TŌJI

This form requires that twelve movements have to be completed in three seconds from the beginning to the end. Omit the movement of raising both hands to the left and the right in the first movement of the basic form, *Manji*-form, and perfect the eight movements in two seconds from the movement of stretching the left hand forward and the right back of the head to Zanshin (see illustration).

THE FORM OF CHOKUSHI

直指の型

2. The form of chokushi

刀字の型

1. 1. The form of toji.

134

剣の持ち方

掌中の剣の位置

第一動。左手の剣を右手でとるところ

「向相の位」（正面）

Koso no I
(from the front)

る。

＜剣のとり方と持ち方＞
左手の剣の中から注意深く右手
に一本の剣をとる。
剣を右手に持ったならば、鷲が
まさにその両翼を開かんとするよ
うな体勢で標的を凝視しながら身
づくろいをする。
＜第一動＞
剣を一本とり、両手をまっすぐ

130

1. The first movement
Taking a blade from the left hand.

2. The way of holding a blade.

3. A position of a blade in the hand.

This form omits further steps from the movements of the form of *Tōji*. At the beginning hold a blade in the right hand and throw in one movement (see illustration).

KŌSŌ NO I (KAMAE) AND WEARING THE SHURIKEN

Although there are *Manji*, *Tōji and* Chokushi forms the position at the moment of throwing is only one. This position is called '*Kōsō no I*' or '*Kōsō no Kamae*'. The photograph is badly damaged but it shows the settled *Kōsō no I* of Master Naruse in front of the target.

Wear a few *shuriken* in front of the side of the abdomen in actual fighting. Beside this you keep the *shuriken* secretly in the right side of the hip or put them in your bosom beneath the right neckband as shown in the illustration.

THE FRONT WAY THROW (JIKISHIN AND URANAMI)

It is normal that as to the front target you aim a *shuriken* at the target facing front as it is shown in the chapter of the basic form, *Kōsō no I*. When the distance between you and the adversary is very short and you haven't time to position yourself in *Kōsō no I*, *Kamae* (position) as the picture shows and then the *Kamae* above the head and throw as if you swing a sword down. In this case, you throw the *shuriken* at either the right foot forward or left foot forward as you like according to the situation.

As to this *Kamae* and the way of throwing since there is not any clear teaching from olden times I call this '*Jikishin*'. In this case it is necessary to hold the *shuriken* with the forefinger over as in the picture.

When you face frontal attack and throw the *shuriken* from below, bend the right knee very low and assume a low posture. Throw the *shuriken* upward from below like the 'Under throw' like a pitcher in baseball. In case you need to assume a lower posture kneel on the right knee and the left foot is in *Tachihiza* (see diagram). When you throw in this posture the *shuriken* flies forward as the wave rolls on. I name this '*Uranami*' because there is not any clear indication about this posture from olden times.

71

1. Za-uchi

2. The sequence of Za-uchi.

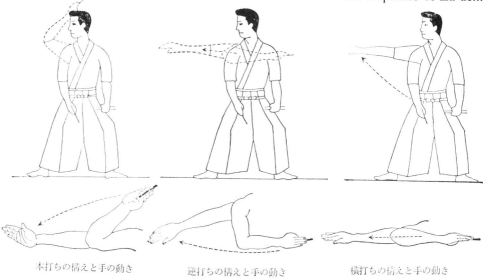

本打ちの構えと手の動き　　　　逆打ちの構えと手の動き　　　　横打ちの構えと手の動き

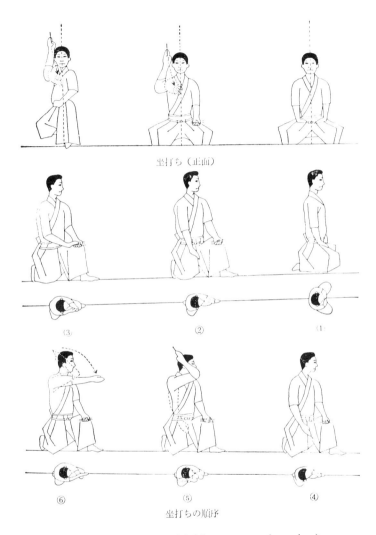

坐打ち（正面）

(3)　　　　　　　　(2)　　　　　　　　(1)

(6)　　　　　　　　(5)　　　　　　　　(4)

坐打ちの順序

3. A – Gyaku-uchi (the reverse throwing)
B – Yoko-uchi (the side way throw)
C – Hon-uchi (throwing towards the right)

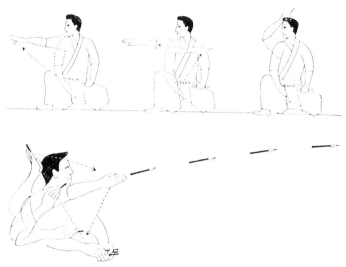

4. Haya-uchi (continuous throwing shuriken)

The method of throwing shuriken as you are walking.

74

THE SIDE WAY THROW

There are three ways of throwing to the right side and to the left.

The first is called *Seijō-uchi* or *Hon-uchi* and throws towards the right like the picture.

The second is *Yoko-uchi*. The *Kamae* is like the picture and throws at the adversary on the left side or the right.

The third is *Gyaku-uchi*, the reverse throwing. This is an under throw to the right side upwards.

THE THROW FROM THE SITTING POSTURE

Generally you throw a *shuriken* from the standing posture 'Tachi-uchi' but if necessary, you throw it from the sitting posture 'Za-uchi'.

This basic training is that you sit upright hold a *shuriken* facing your adversary in the right hand above the right back of the head and throw. There is the other way of throwing. You position the left leg *Tachihiza* (as diagram), kneel on the right heel with legs wide open and throw. This way is easier than the before mentioned way. (See the illustration).

When you throw with this form separately, to begin with, sit upright facing the target with your *shuriken* in the left hand. Then position yourself with the target in the left. The left leg is in *Hizadachi*, put the right foot on tiptoe and put it under the right buttock. During this movement it is essential that your eyes are fixed on the target, making sure your navel is pointing at the bull's eye. Transfer the *shuriken* from the left hand to the right hand; when you have the *shuriken* in the right hand lower the hand by the right thigh and once more make sure your navel is pointing at the bull's eye. Position the *shuriken* above the right back of the head and throw.

To your adversary from the side you throw with *Hon-uchi, Yoko-uchi* and *Gyaku-uchi* in the sitting posture (see the illustration).

The first *shuriken* with *Hon-uchi*, the second, *Yoko-uchi*, the third *Uranami*, but in this case it is difficult to throw with *Uranami*. As before mentioned (the left leg is in *Hizadachi*), position the right leg as in *Hizadachi*.

HAYA-UCHI

In *shuriken* you have to win the battle with the first *shuriken* but it is necessary to train to throw the next *shuriken* quickly.

A strong adversary may receive your first *shuriken* well, but you must watch for a chance and throw the second *shuriken*. This is, before the first *shuriken* hits the target the second and third *shuriken* have to follow continuously. This *Haya-uchi* won't give any chance to the adversary to regain his footing, let alone advance.

From olden times it is said '*Ikki-Goken*' that is, to throw five *shuriken* in one breath. We have to aim for that.

HOW TO THROW SHURIKEN AS YOU ARE WALKING

When an adversary attacks you from the right side turn your whole body to the right and you may throw with *Hon-uchi (Seijō-uchi)*, but this takes time; you should throw with *Gyaku-uchi* (see diagram).

If the adversary attacks twist your body to the left back and throw with *Gyaku-uchi* (see the illustration.

TŌJUTSU KUMIKOMI NO KATA – THE POSITION COMBINES THE SHUR-IKEN ART WITH THE ART OF THE SWORD

This is also called '*Tōjutsu Heiyō no Kata*'. This form shows how to throw *shuriken* as if you are fighting with a sword. Altogether there are five possibilities for *shuriken*. It is said that especially the fourth (*shuriken*) position came from Miyamoto Musashi's position with which he defeated Shishido Baiken who fought with Kusarigama (a sickle and chain) against Musashi's *shuriken*.

(The First *shuriken*)

Wear five *shuriken* in front of the right side and hold up a sword with the right hand. After salutation pass the sword to the left hand and wear it. After tucking in the *Sageo* (a sword knot) into one's *obi* (a sash), begin the first form.

Hold the *Sayaguchi* (the mouth of the scabbard) with the left hand and hold the

A. the first shuriken.

B. the second shuriken.

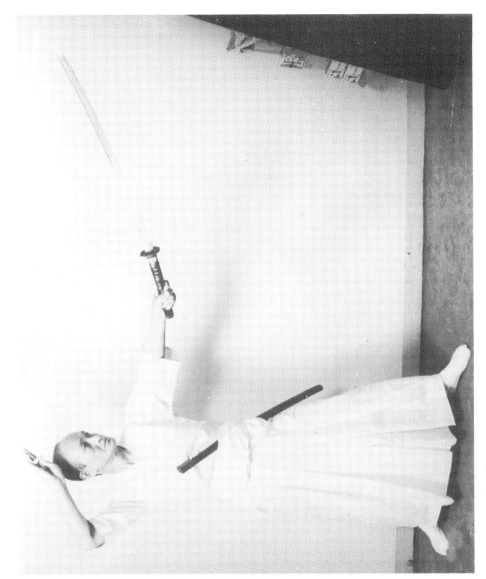

C. the third shuriken.

D. the fourth shuriken.

E. the fifth shuriken.

handle 1.5cm below the *Tsuba* (sword guard) with the right hand; put out the right foot about 30cm forward diagonally. At the same time you draw out the sword, position the sword in one hand *Hasso* and step back on the right foot to your former position. This is, parallel with the handle to the arm and position on the right side. Stand in an upright posture and fix one's eyes on the target holding Saya-guchi (the mouth of scabbard) in your left hand.

Next, pass the sword to your left hand, Kamae, draw a shuriken with the right hand, lower the hand to the right side. During all these movements you have to fix your eyes on the target.

Step forward to the target, give a shout '*Ya*', with all your might at the appropriate distance. *Kamae* the sword *Hidari-te Jōdan* (see the picture), and with the *shuriken* as a rule, and close in upon your adversary by inches with *Hidari-Hanshin* (the left half of the body forward). This *Kokyu* (timing) is very important and we call this '*In ni Komoru*'.

This *Kamae* of *Hidari-Jodan*, positioning the sword high above the left side, is very unusual.

As you are full of spirit and have struck the *shuriken*, *Kamae* the sword in *Hasso*-posture at once. Keep the sword in both hands attaching the end of the handle slightly to the lower abdomen, hold it horizontally, the point of the sword forward.

Your left foot should be drawn back left diagonally about 30cm. Stretch your right arm forward, hold the mouth of the scabbard and prepare for '*Nōtō*', putting a sword in the scabbard.

Fixing the eyes on the target put away the sword steadily, take a firm hold of the mouth of the scabbard with the left hand, return the left leg to the previous position and finish in a natural posture.

The Second

Holding out the sword vertically in the left hand, throw a *shuriken*. At this time aim the right side of the sword guard at the space between the eyes of the adversary.

The Third

Holding out *Kirisaki* of the sword, on the left hand side forward in the left hand, throw a *shuriken*. At this time, *Kirisaki*, the point of the sword is to be aimed at the space between the eyes of the adversary.

The Fourth

Holding out *Kirisaki* of the sword, lower on the left hand side forward in the left hand, throw a *shuriken* (one of the fourth) or, there is the other way. Holding out the sword at the head of the handle to the left, *Kirisaki* to the right, throw a *shuriken* (two of the fourth).

The Fifth

Without drawing a sword, position the handle diagonally in front of you and throw (one of the fifth). At the moment you have finished a throw draw the sword quickly, hold it horizontally, the handle to the right and *Kirisaki* to the left (two of the fifth), then hold it out forward and put it in the scabbard.

Beside these five throws the other throws '*Inken*' are to be added. The first throw can be followed continuously by a rather small sized *shuriken* hidden in the sword handle or hidden in one's *Hachimaki* headband, in the sleeve or in the bosom.

There are others such as *Zengo-uchi* (a throw of the front and back) and *Shiho-uchi* (a throw to all sides).

WOMEN AND SHURIKEN

Master Naruse taught *shuriken* to 15 year old girl students at the Shizuoka High School. *Shuriken* is a very suitable martial art for women, so I will relate a few stories about women and *shuriken*.

'THE REVENGE OF MIYAGINO AND HER SISTER'

In the village of Sakato in the territory Katakura Kojuro, the head of Shiraishi Sendai Ōshiu, a peasant called Yotaro was weeding a rice field with his two daughters. Katakura's retainer, Shiga Danshichi, happened to pass just as one of the daughters threw a muddy weed to the footpath between the rice fields. The weed hit Danshichi in the face, and being in a bad humour, he cut the father Yotaro in two at the single stroke of his sword, though the older man had begged his pardon. The two sisters made up their minds to avenge their father and went all the way to Tokyo to gain Yui Shosetsu's help. Shosetsu took them in, and named them Miyagino and Nobuo. He then taught the elder sister *shuriken* and the younger sister Naginata or halberd. After three years they had mastered the technique, but he let them train for a further two years and then entered into *Sendai* and applied for their revenge in public. The government had pity on their filial piety and fixed a date when they could take their revenge at the castle town. Miyagino avoided the sword with which Danshichi slashed at her to his right, fending it off at her left. Danshichi was off guard, and Miyagino threw out a *shuriken* which stuck in his right eye. Danshichi faltered and seemed to lose heart, but still showered blows everywhere in desperation. Miyagino, seizing her opportunity, swung the blade, they exchanged blows but at last she got a grip around both his hands as she called "Nobuo, Nobuo." Nobuo ran up and cut off his arm, and Miyagino immediately said: "Merciful Buddha! We have slain Shiga Danshichi, the sworn enemy of our late father. Now let him ascend to heaven". So saying she cut of Danshichi's head."

Master Naruse had done research into this story and there is evidence to support it. For example, the place of the revenge was Roppon Matsu Monbara, a Shiraishi town of which traces are still left. In the fourteenth year of Taisho (1926) at the Sakato village of that time (nowadays it is the Otakasawa village of Karita-gun, Miyagi-Ken) it was decided to build a monument and the next year it was completed in April, the fifteenth year of Taisho. It was given the name '*Kōshido*', the monument of dutiful daughters.

I have heard that Mr Shimura, who is a descendant of the sisters' father, Yotaro, and ten other people had an exhibition of the weapons used, and read the deposition left by the departed, and some 123 other records.

'SHURIKEN OYAE TALE'

In the Kanei period (1624-1644) at Ushikunuma there was a deaf ferryman at the ferry of the Mito highway. One day a *ronin* (masterless *samurai* or *bushi*) called the ferry back as it neared the centre of the river. But the ferryman, unhearing, continued across. Thinking that he was being ignored , the *ronin* threw a *shuriken* which glanced off the surface of the water struck the neck of the old ferryman and killed him.

Now the old man had a daughter, Oyae. Determining to avenge herself on her father's murderer, she trained in *shuriken* with the help of the headman of the village. When the training had passed she was 18 years old and very beautiful. As one of the ways to seek her foe, she appeared as a tumbler at the show tent at Hiro Kōji, Ryōgoku, Edo. The tent was always full because she was so highly praised as an expert in *shuriken*.

One day, Shuzei, son of Hikosaka Unai, who was a master of the spear and a retainer of Honda Chumu Dayu , saw the technique and was much impressed with it. He saw that she was more than just a tumbler and asked the reason. Then he asked his father to look after her at their house. Shuzei let her strike with white fans instead of *shurikens* while he fought with a dagger and long sword. Although he knocked down a few of the fans, he was finally hit by one of them that struck his neck. His father was watching this as if to say "Oh, my son was unmanly". Taking a *yari* (spear), he let her use a real blade. Her right arm had been caught by his spear before she had a chance to position a blade, "Oh, Oyeae! Your technique is splendid, but you know only how to attack but not how to defend. Now, learn the art of the *Ko-dachi* (a small *tachi*) and take revenge for your father's death with this technique and attain your long cherished object". Oyae learned the art of *Ko-dachi* (a small *Tachi*) and made rapid progress. Then she worked on the military art of free offence, and defence with the *Ko-dachi* in her left hand and a *shuriken* in her right hand. Now Akasawa Genpachi, a *ronin* of the *Tsugaru-han* came to ask for a job as a *shuriken* expert with Lord Honda. Investigation found that he had been the murderer of the girl's father ten years before. Hikosaka Unai informed his lord of the details, and it was decided to let her avenge her father's death and obtain her long cherished object before the lord. To this end, they decoyed him out under the name of a *shuriken* match in the lord's presence.

As Genpachi let ten *shuriken*s stand close together at a round board target, Oyae threw ten stones and drove each *shuriken*'s head in from four to five steps farther than Genpachi; and taking one more stone, she threw it at the board so that the *shuriken*s fell off. Lord Honda said in a loud voice: "Both of you are splendid! Now fight each other, fight with real *shuriken*". Genpachi was secretly afraid but he received the annoucement with apparent nonchalance and soon the two of them faced each other with one *shuriken* each. Oyae held the *shuriken* which had been stuck in her father's neck in her right hand over her head and took *Ko-dachi* in her left hand. "Mezurashiya Genpachi!" she said, declaring her name in due form. "Now kill a would-be avenger!" He replied, striking a blow which should have transfixed her throat. For a moment it seemed that Oyae was in danger, but she struck down the blade like lightning with the *Ko-dachi* in her left hand and simultaneously, the rusted *shuriken* in her right hand had flown and pierced his throat through. Genpachi stood still for a moment, then fell dead, the blade was stuck in the same place in the neck where her father had received his death-stroke.

MODERN WOMEN AND THE SHURIKEN ART

As I mentioned before, *shuriken* was one of the martial arts suitable for women as were *Ko-dachi* and *naginata*. I think *shuriken* is also suitable for modern women since it is the best method of self defence against evil doers as well as training mind and body. It occurred to me to try teaching *shuriken* to women only. I placed an advertisement. "*Shuriken* teaching: for women only" in women's weekly magazines. At the time I thought that it would be wonderful if even ten women wished to learn it and that a least a few of them would continue it at the very best. I was to be surprised. The day after the advertisement appeared, my mailbox was full of letters from places as distant as Hokkaido in the north and Kyushu in the south. There were over 250 applications, and their questions were varied indeed: "I want to learn *shuriken*"; "I am living in Kyushu. If I train every day, how long will it take to learn the outline of *shuriken*? If necessary, I will come up to Tokyo". Or. "I am going to Brazil, and would like to learn *shuriken* for self defence."

But I couldn't welcome 200 women into a *dōjo* of six mats. To begin with, if two hundred women all threw *shuriken* at once, what would happen? At the least, several police cars would come and I would become the cause of public concern. Life, I felt acutely, doesn't flow evenly. So I told those who lived far away or were not able to come to training to wait. I eventually chose ten women among the applicants and began the classes.

Before I met them, I wondered what sort of women would come... Who would like to learn the out-dated art of *shuriken* which seems odd in this age of rapid progress and the constant appearance of new things. I thought that they were probably inquisitive young ladies who found time heavy on their hands and that if I trained them a little hard, they would disappear like smoke. But these preconceptions were completely shattered when I met them the first time. All were attractive. They included the head of staff of a first class company, a pianist, a violinist, and a designer of precision machines. I coached them hard in accordance with the old rule, a hard *Gyō* (training), not only for modern men, but even for the *bushi*. Blades are thrown at a straw-mat target several hundred times, then a thousand times, two thousand times. Even in training we use real blades so we must always be on guard, ready to dodge swiftly or catch the blade in the air. This training was really done well by the women and I was pleased from my heart to find these women among so many thoughtless creatures strutting around today.

Shuriken was a very individual martial art among the old *bushi* from the point of view that we could defeat an opponent with a tiny blade. Also, because it is a technique in which we fight to the last drop of our blood, the blade and the mind must always be in the same state. The coincidence of the spirit of sword and of zen is particularly called for.

As long as we do not concentrate in throwing, the blade does not work well. Thus, our mental state clearly shows in the striking of the blade. *Shuriken* is the barometer of a mental state. I can always test my mental concentration by throwing a blade. But to achieve this state, we have to continue simple training with patience; and only someone who stands the hard fundamental training can master the *shuriken* art. It is already thirty years since I started training, but I have not reached the secret yet. Yet I mastered the techinque and continued to train my mind until at least I can manage to strike a 'live' blade. With that, I gained confidence in myself and my way of life. I have already told how the student to whom I taught *shuriken* changed from an idler to a capable man, being given true self-confidence by *shuriken*. Here is the evidence that the art of *shuriken* is still alive now.

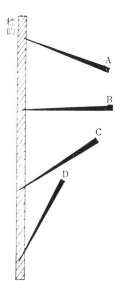

SHURIKEN AND THE MIND

It is very difficult to put one's heart and soul into one thing. Much patience and passion are both needed. The boy I told about changed himself through the training of *shuriken*, ceasing to spend time in poor company and becoming a capable engineer because of his patience and drive.

As I wrote before, there is a strict religious morality connected with the Martial Arts. When I taught the boy *shuriken*, I made sure that he kept his promise – which he did very well. I told him that he had to banish worldly thoughts from his mind when he threw a blade. A dishonest person must not be allowed to handle a blade, lest that blade turn evil. I learned through my own experience that as long as we throw a blade correctly and calmly, it will fly correctly.

THE MARVELLOUS COINCIDENCE THAT THE WAY OF SWORDSMANSHIP COINCIDES WITH THE WAY OF ZEN

YAMAOKA TESSHU

As I grew up in war time, I usually bore the subject of 'death' in mind. Since I was weak from my boyhood, I faced death several times and was particularly interested in the subject. Even as a child I had thought that I would like to be a 'man who does not fear death'. At the time, the word *hara* was popular with the public. 'Someone with plenty of guts', or 'training hara', were popular expressions.

My father had never sat in religious meditation nor had he done training, but he often talked about Zen and he hunted out and read Zen books. I believe that he thought about learning Zen to train in '*hara*' and not as a religion. I was influenced by him and practiced Zen meditation at the meetings in the *Zuien* temple near my home in *Sendagaya* and joined the Session of *Enkaku* Temple in *Kamakura* while I was a student. Unnoticed, the secrets of Zen and the secrets of swordsmanship coincided. We should aim to reach the state of the coincidence of *Ken-Zen* (sword and Zen). My early thoughts on this must have been influenced by the books, '*Miyamoto Musashi*' by Yoshikawa Eiji; '*Gorin-no-sho*' '*Dokodo*' written by Musashi; and '*Kamakura Bushi-to-Zen*'. Yamaoka Tesshu Koji was my ideal; one whose world was one of the coincidence of *Ken-Zen*. He was very well-known as a *kensei* or saint of the sword between the end of the Tokugawa Shogunate and Meiji.

I have come to believe that even if we learn *shuriken* we not only have to complete the technique, but we also have to enter the way of the heart by which we overcome the technique. The clear ideal for me was Yamaoka Tesshu. He mentioned the process of his training in the martial arts as follows: 'I aimed to be a swordsman at nine years of age. I learned under Kusumi Kenteki-sai of the *Shinkage-ryu* after which I trained under Inoue Kiyotora of *Hokushin Itto-ryu*. I fought ruffians of other schools more than several ten thousands.

For those times, for twenty years I worked hard, but had not yet attained peace of mind. I had sought everywhere for an expert in swordsmanship, but had yet to find one. By chance I heard that there was such a man, Asari Matashichiro of the *Itto-ryu*, the second son of Nakanishi Chuta who succeeded in the tradition of Ito Ittosai. Pleased, I went and asked for a fight. his technique was very different from the swordsmanship which is in worldly fashion. It appears delicate from the outside, but is indeed hard on the inside and he 'breathed with one being' and knew his chances of victory before attack. So should a Master be. Whenever I fought him I knew that he was far beyond me. I never neglected my training, but there was no way to defeat him.

Afterwards, when I practised the sword with other people day by day, I had only to think of Asari and he stood before me at once, like an unscaleable mountain.

On the 13th of May in the 13th year of *Meiji (1880)*, early one morning in my bedroom, I imagined I was to fight Asari with a sword as usual – but this time his vision did not appear. Here, I mastered the mystery of invincibility. I invited Asari to examine me, which he kindly did, and praised my skills. I announced the art I had developed, calling it the *Muto* (no sword)-*ryū*.

Oh! training in other ways goes likewise. Our men of old said that if you really put your heart into training you will reach your goal – never neglect your lessons.

For ten years I practiced the way of the sword and revised my thoughts. At last I gained freedom and defended it even more. But there came a day when I broke and threw away that defence and all fortified positions. I felt then more perfection than ever before, as if my heart were full to the brim with early morning mist."

When I read the biography of Yamaoka Tesshu, I realised that I had found the master whose 'coincidence of *Ken-Zen*' was my ideal. Although I knew that the making of that great man was very different from mine, I was overjoyed to confirm my purpose, and to determine that I would make my way in *Shuriken* and *Zen* to the best of my ability.

I felt as though Miyamoto Musashi was still alive, and found myself thinking that perhaps I could travel all around Japan, meet a master tactician, and receive more training.

It was war time; I thought that on the battle field I would fight to the death with all the skills that were now at my command.

At any rate, the *shuriken* art is very unique amongst *kobudō* because the weapon is a small blade with which one defeats an adversary. Especially as it is a 'waza' which is used at the risk of one's life, the blade and mind must be one. Here the spirit of *zen-ken* has been stressed.

As I mentioned many times, when you are irritated and not satisfied, if you throw a blade so as to satisfy your resentment, the blade flies disorderly because you do not have the correct attention. If you do not concentrate on throwing the blade, the blade will not have a life; your state of mind appears on the way it strikes the target. *Shuriken* is a barometer of one's state of mind. When one is free from worldly thoughts you will achieve an alive strike and your anger and irritation will have disappeared. The strike of the blade is then ever better.

By throwing a blade I try to concentrate my mind when I feel uneasy. I sit facing the target and calm down and throw a blade. Once you regain your presence of mind you can strike the target as you like. To reach this state you have to continue the simple training patiently.

At the time when I became a pupil of master Naruse he talked about this. It is easy to start but it is hard to achieve it. Step by step you have to train your art and spirit. Only a person who goes through hardness is able to reach the true spirit of *shuriken*. I looked up to Tesshu as my mentor of my mind, my other master was Shirai Tōru.

TENSHIN ITTŌ RYU

Shirai Tōru, the founder of the Shirai-Ryu *shuriken* style, whom I respect as he is not only the founder of my school but also my senior; he persevered in the way of the sword.

In a lot of stories great swordsmen are described as if they had no rivals in the world since they were born, of course, there would be such swordsmen but for me the most interesting subject is in what way they attained their great art and their state of mind.

Shirai Tōru was born into the family of a clansman in Bizen Okayama in the 3rd year of Tenmei (1783). At the age of eight he became a pupil of Ida Shinpachiro of the

Kijin-ryu. When he was fourteen he went to Edo (Tokyo) and was admitted to the school of Nakanishi Chūtu Shikei. He was the third generation of the Nakanishi group of the Ittō-ryu and said to be one of the prominent swordsmen in Edo. It was the 15th of January, the 9th of Kansei (1798). After his death Shirai Tōru trained under the fourth generation, Nakanishi Chubei Komasa. He trained desperately every day regardless of snow, rain or ill-health. He brandished a wooden sword and practised his *kiai* always until midnight. Thus he became a leading swordsman of his school and at his age twenty three he left his master to go back to his home town, Okayama.

Then he opened a *dōjō* and taught swordsmen in his town. It was the time when people admired that 'lights spurted out of the tip of his sword.'

His fame gradually spread, especially as he had his own art 'Hassun no Kyokushaku', so as to learn the art more than three hundred people came to him. During his staying there for six years his name resounded throughout the neighbourhood, but he gradually became skeptical about his swordsmanship. Whenever he saw a wane in the art of his senior swordsmen he remembered that once they were better than him and he had looked up to them. It made him think about his own future as a swordsman. Does only the strength of swordsmanship and the art exist when they are in their prime? It is just the same strength as a wild beast or a fighting cock?

It was very hard to accept that the way of swordsmanship was like that. His ideal swordsmanship must be different. There is no any way of facing an enemy with serenity and of controlling the enemy even when his youth has gone. His mind was troubled and he fell into deep skepticism.

He went to Edo again to find some answer. It was the 3rd year of Bunka (1806). He visited Terada Munenari, the senior at his school where Shirai trained when he came to Edo for the first time. Tōru was twenty nine years old and in his prime, on the contrary Terada was an aged man of sixty three years old. As soon as Terada heard about his junior's earnest doubt, he urged him to take a wooden sword and stand in the center of the *dōjō*. Shirai bowed and faced Terada and he was thinking, "Once Terada trained me as my senior and I stared in wonder at his art, but now he is old and I have had hard training in *Okayama*."

At the moment he stood with a sword waiting to close with him. After several years absence he felt that his self-confidence in swordsmanship fell into pieces. Terada advanced calmly holding up his sword. It was as if a great mountain was closing up on him. Tōru was overpowered by the tip of Terada's sword, he found no place for his hands and feet and was perspiring. Suddenly the picture of his own face flashed across his mind and he remembered the admiration of the other swordsmen in his home town, who said that lights spurted from the tip of his sword. It was a perfect defeat.

He felt a touch of an answer to his question when he was controlled thoroughly by an old swordsman aged sixty-five.

"I am very much obliged to you, you are beyond my reach." He admired Terada's art as he was hoping that one word from his senior might solve his earnest quest. "Why is your swordsmanship so skilful?" he asked expectantly.

"You have attained a certain good stage, but there will be no success without spirituality being awakened in you." He spoke quietly and left the *dōjō*. Since then he trained hard but he could not reach the satisfactory state of mind. At a loss he visited Terada again.

"You have gone astray for twenty years, you are obsessed with a distracting idea. You have to release this properly. Unless you perform your ablution every day and become pure you will not be able to reach spiritual awareness."

For his way of swordsmanship he decided not to be afraid of death he persevered in his training and ablutions at home or on a journey regardless of rainy mornings and snowy mornings, and windy nights and frosty nights, he devoted himself solely to his search. Thus five years passed, he grew weaker and it looked as if the clouds of doubt covered his heart.

By chance he had heard of 'Naikan no hō', the law of inner reflection. He felt as if he saw a light on a moonless night and devoted himself to this law. Not only his body and mind recover day by day, he became full of energy and swiftness in his skill. Although he knew that Terada was beyond his reach he visited his senior and told him his situation.

"You have advanced well, now you had better meet Tokumoto, the ascetic for further help." Terada was pleased and gave this advice.

Shirai followed the advice he went to the *dōjō* and spent days in the sound of chanting Buddhist invocations and the temple bell. One day when he was watching the holy priest chanting as he was hitting the bell, he became awakened. A large change came over his mind. The hand of the holy priest was not moving in order to move, Tōru saw clearly his movement and the sound of chanting was in one with the secret of heaven. There was no movement in order to move, no sound to chant, no awakening, nor doubt, besides, he was in there not as an observer but as himself. His illusions were

93

banished at the same time he felt awakened. But nothing was added to him, nor lost, he was filled with an inexplicable joy. By way of experiment he took up his sword and he saw that his art reflected his fine feeling as if he were another person.

At last he realised that the essence of perfection in his art was not merely dependent on his skill but on his state of mind, the power would never wane. It is not necessary to mention Terada's congratulations. Shirai was in another state. There was no comparison with Terada, nor victory over him.

I cannot help being moved by his ardent search whenever I perform the *shuriken* of the Shirai-ryu in a moonless night by myself I remember his spirit. Assuming Shirai's search, once more I think about the way of the flying *shuriken* a new deep emotion arises in me.

Regardless of the blade everything flies as it turns, the hardest part of *shuriken* is how to control this turning to fly straight and hit a target. The Negishi-ryu, Shindo-ryu, and other schools spared no pains to control this turning and finally they reached the idea of changing centre of gravity of *shuriken*. On the contrary the art of *shuriken* of the Shirai-ryu with Shirai Tōru as its leader, invented the way of displaying its nature more than enough without opposing the force of nature. I think that this way well-expresses Shirai's state of spirit. At the end he devoted himself in nature and discovered swordsmanship in nature. Because of this he added the two characters of Tenshin to the name of Ittō-ryu in which he trained, and expressed his own world by calling it Tenshin Ittō-ryu.

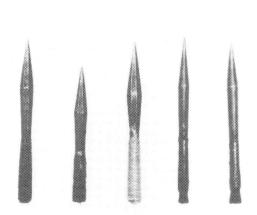

A-H, Shuriken of the Negishi-ryu.

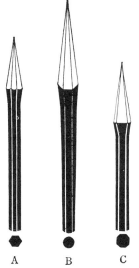

A   B   C

根岸流の手裏剣

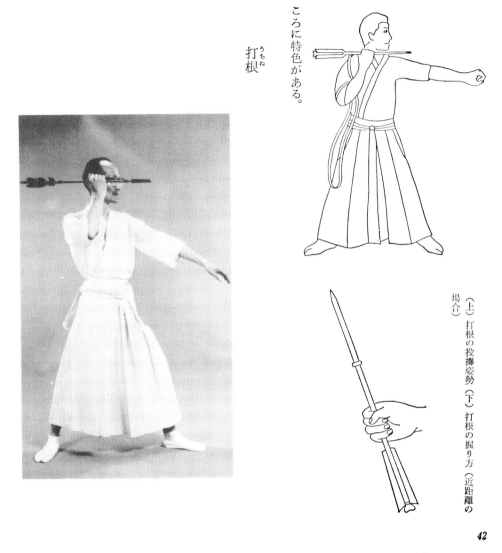

打根
うちね

（上）打根の投擲姿勢　（下）打根の握り方　（近距離の場合）

42

1. The throwing posture of uchine.
2. The way of holding an uchine (for a short distance.)

JAPANESE THROWING ART

INJI-UCHI OR INJI

How have the throwing weapons and the art of throwing developed in Japan? In very early times throwing stones were used. For example, they are mentioned in '*Heike Monogatari*' and '*Yoshitune-ki*'. Throwing stones were called '*Inju-uchi*' or '*Inji*'. There were warriors whose duty it was to throw stones. They were called '*Inji-no-Kanjya*' or '*Mukaireki-no-mono*'. About the time of Emperor Juntoku (He reigned 1210-1221), in the scene of '*Nenjyu-gyōji Inari Matsuri*' (the annual god, the fox god, of harvest festival) painted by Tosa Mitsunari, a man is seen thowing a stone with a tool which is similar to the implements used by the Incas and called by them a *honda*. We can tell then that even in our country the stone was not only thrown by the hand but also with the tool.

'Nenjyu-gyōji Inari Matsuri'

It is interesting that the sharp-eyed painter drew the posture of the two men in this picture in the fundamental posture of *Shuriken*.

At a later date, the Edo era (1600-1867) came. In '*Kaikoku-Heidan*' (a maritime country tale) by Hayashi Shihei a picture entitled, '*Netherlander practising throwing a stone*' is described. It shows them throwing stones, which are kept in a bag on their shoulder, with *honda*, at a target which looks like a doll's head. It suddenly occurred to me that anything which a human being does stands apart from time and space and remains ever the same. Elsewhere in the world besides Tokyo, demonstrators can be seen to throw stones, but I have never seen them using *hondas*. At this point, whilst talking about the art of throwing, it can be said that our ancestors were better than the people today.

JAVELIN THROWING

In the development of the throwing art of the world, the art of throwing stones developed firstly in the *Honda* system and then progressed to throwing bars instead of stones, later it became javelin throwing, a weapon which pierces to death. Javelin throwing was quite popular elsewhere in Europe as well as in Greece and Rome.

In Japan javelin throwing was not developed as a separate art. The javelin was used to spear rather than to throw. However within the art of javelin used in Japan for spearing there was a minor section devoted to the use of throwing weapons called *uchine* which was like a javelin but much smaller.

Next we must consider the position of the feet of a javelin thrower. The tips of the toes of the left foot should be directly in line with the target. Similarly the heel of the right foot should be in a straight line. By standing in this position, when one throws a javelin and consequently twists the body, the target and the centre of the body are in a straight line. Although I have already mentioned this before when writing about the *Shuriken*, when throwing a *Shuriken*, one stands with the big toes of the left and right feet in line with the target. The difference in the stance of the javelin thrower and a *Shuriken* thrower is that the *kamae* of a *Shuriken* is nearer to the centre line than the other (that is, slightly above the right side of the head).

UCHI-NE

There is also another kind of small hand-spear used in throwing called *uchi-ne*. It resembles a thick arrow, is thrown by hand, not by a bow, and is sometimes thrust direct into one's enemy. Sometimes strings are fastened to a hole halfway down the shaft made of bamboo, and in order to throw it again, the strings are pulled back and then released: thus it can be used again and again. There are three or four sets of feathers attached, as on an arrow. This method of throwing is identical to the *Kamae* of javelin throwing for covering long distances. For short distances, you hold it like in the illustration and throw.

HISTORY OF THE SHURIKEN ART AND THE SCHOOLS

I would now like to write about the history of *Shuriken* and about the *Waza* (technique) and the essence of the nine centimetre sword which my ancestors originated in its entirety.

THE ORIGIN OF SHURIKEN

Before the *shuriken* other weapons that were thrown were stones, javelins and *uchine*. The actual *shuriken* was devised at the time of Meiwa and Anei (1764-1781) during the Tokugawa era by Katōno Hirohide of the *Sendai-han*.

In fact the acts of throwing *shuriken*-like objects have been practised since ancient times for example, in the *Kojiki* (Ancient Shinto Myths) there is an account of Prince Yamato-Takeru's returning from the conquest of the east. He was a Prince, a son of the Emperor Kageyuki. "Prince Yamato-Takeru, after persuading the wild Ainu to submit to him, went to make peace with the wild gods of the mountain and rivers. On his way back, a wicked god of the slope appeared in the disguise of a white deer where the Prince was having a meal at the foot of mount Ashigara. The Prince was eating a *hiru* which he threw, striking the deer in the eye and causing him to die." – Iwanami Bunko, Page 124. (A *hiru* is a vegetable about 2.0 or 2.4 cm wide with a hard bulb like a scallion.) His action describes well enough the main points of the *shuriken* art.

There is also an account of the Emperor Suiko (554-628) in '*Nihon Shoki*'; amongst the presents he received from Korai (part of the Korean dynasty) was a weapon, the *Ishihajiki*. The *Ishihajiki* is a stone-throwing instrument. Again mentioned in a *Choka* (long poem) of Manyoshu in the 13th volume: '…thrown an arrow, it has receded into the distance…' From this passage it would seem that the art of arrow throwing has been practised from early times. Apart from these, and before the *shuriken* was established, the sword, dagger, *wakizashi*, etc., were being thrown as the javelin and arrow.

THE APPEARANCE OF SHURIKEN

It is written in the '*Osaka Gunki*' (the military record of the Osaka states) as follows: 'Ogasawara Tadamasa was thrust back by a javelin. But Tadamasa saved himself from his foe by drawing out a *wakizashi* (short sword) and throwing it, as you would a *shuriken*, at his enemy. The attacker lost heart and withdrew his javelin.' In the '*Jozan Kidan*' (the interesting stories of Jozan Kidan), it is said that 'Yoshihiro donned his armour, sewn together with black leather, and a helmet decorated with bear's fur on the *shikoro* (neck piece) and crossed long swords with Inoue. Yoshihiro was knocked down from his horse, but saved himself by drawing out a *wakizashi* and hitting his opponent with this, as if it were a *shuriken*.

Later Ogasawara Tadamasa created the pure *shuriken*, the *Tantō-gata shuriken* which had the shape of a short sword. They are as in the illustration.

Shuriken is a military art originating from actual fighting during the Civil Wars in the early part of the Tokugawa era. Although warriors threw stones, javelins, arrows, swords and daggers, gradually one type of sword was used exclusively. This *shuriken* became a weapon by incorporating the function of the arrow, flying stick and the sword thrust, and was devised to be especially fit for throwing by hand.

At first, the shape of the sword and the method used for throwing it did not conform to any particular standard, but gradually it became uniform and the various schools were established.

THE SCHOOL AND THE SHAPE OF THE SWORD

Shuriken is often thought of as a kind of *kozuka* or knife that is held upside down with the blade pointing towards the person holding it. But these are used as substitutes for *shuriken* and this method of throwing is just one of many. If this is so, what is a real *shuriken*? It is very difficult to give a simple answer to this question since as in other martial arts, there are diverse schools, and the shapes of blades and the various methods of throwing them must be considered.

As part of the history of *Shuriken*, I think this is the time to mention the representatives of the school of *shuriken* art in Japan, the type of swords used, and the way to throw them.

The names of these schools have been handed down from ancient times as follows:–

THE NAMES OF THE SCHOOLS AND THE ORIGINATORS

Schools	Originators
Asayama Ichiden ryū	*Asayama Ichidensai Shigetoyo*
Tenshin ryu	*Tenshin Kogenta*
Araki ryu	*Araki Mujin sai Minamoto no Hidetsuna*
Iga ryu	
Izu ryu	
Ikkan ryu	*Katono izu Hirohide*
Enmei ryu	*Shibuki Shinjurō*
Onko Chishin ryu	*Miyamoto Musashi Shomei*
Kasuga ryu	*Hirazumi Heikurō Masamitsu*
Katōno ryu	
Katorishintō ryu	*Katono Izu Hirohide*
Ganritsu ryu or Gan ryu	*Iishino Chōisai Ienao*
Kusaka ryu	*Shorin Sama no suke Eikichi*
Koga ryu	*Kusaka Kazutoshi*
Koden ryu	
Kobori ryu	*Fujiwara no Kamatari*
Shishin ryu	*Kobori Kankaiyu Nyudōsho Kiyohira Yoshiyuki*
Jitsuyō ryu	
Shoshō ryu	*Masugi Saburōzaemon Mitsuoki*
Shōsetsu ryu	*Hirayama Kōzōsen*
Shirai ryu or Tenshinden Itto ryu	*Iwasa Yagozaemon Kiyozumi*
Shinkage ryu	*Dogawa Ninnaemon Munechika*
Shingetsu ryu	*Yui Minbu no suke Tachibana Shosetsu*

Shinshin ryu	*Shirai Tōru Toshikane*
Shintō shobu ryu	*Sodatoyogoro Kagetomo*
Seishin ryu	*Fujiwara Naritada*
Daitō ryu	*Sekiguchi Hachiroemon Ujikiyo*
Takeuchi Ishin ryu	*Ogasawara Shirō no suke Nagamasa*
Takemura ryu	*Mori Kasuminosuke Shigekatsu*
Tatsumi ryu	*Sekiguchi Hachiroemon Ujikiyo*
Chishin ryu	*Ogasawara Shiro no suke Nagamasa*
Tsugawa ryu	*Mōri Kasumi no suke Shigekatsu*
Ten ryu	*Sekiguchi Hachiroemon Ujikiyo*
Niwaori	*Takeda Sokaku*
Negishi ryu	*Shinohara Shigeuemon Ishinsai*
Hozan ryu	*Takemura Yoemon Noritoshi*
Heishu ryu	*Tatsumi Sanykō*
Matsu ryu	*Iijima Ichibei*
Miuraryu	
Shodō ryu	*Sue Jeumon*
Yoshio ryu	*Niwaori E Ujitomo*
Mōen ryu	*Neigshi Chuzo Noriyoshi Shorei*
Negoro ryu	*Tsutsumi Ymashiro no kami Hōzan*
Bukyoku ryu	
Yamauchi ryu	*Nakano Hansui Kagetatsu*
Yuwa ryu	*Miura nobukiyo*

From 'The Illustrations of the *Shuriken* Art' by Fujita Saiko.

Amongst these schools some teach *shuriken* exclusively, others include *shuriken* with swordsmanship. For some we have the name of the tradition only.

101

THE MAIN SCHOOLS

Soratobu Kenshi (Ganritsu-ryu) – (The Swordsman Flying in the Sky)

This school was founded by Matsubayashi Henyasai who came from Matsushiro in Shinano, and was commonly known as Sama-no-suke Hisayoshi. He served under the 18th lord of Matsushiro in Kanei 20th (about 1624).

He was a proficient swordsman and had the artistic name of Ganritsu. He had a trick when facing an opponent of springing in every direction. Quite often his clothes brushed again the eaves of the house. People admired him because he could 'fly' as if he were a bat. Because of this he earned another nickname, Henyasai.

Someone told him a story about Yoshitsune Genkuro, who amused himself by cutting a twig of willow. Although he cut the end of this twig into eight, it still did not fall into the water. When Ganritsu heard this tale, he exclaimed, "I can do that". He performed this feat in front of another person and only after he had cut the end of the twig thirteen times did it finally fall onto the water.

He was so devoted to the art of swordsmanship that there are many stories told about him. For example, every morning without fail he would draw his sword one thousand times! In the last year of his life, he became ill, and his group of disciples were nursing him. One day he suddenly raised his head and said, "Raise me up for I cannot foresake my daily lesson". With one voice the disciples replied, "How about giving it up while you are ill?" But he replied, "No, I cannot give it up". So he drew out his sword one thousand times with the help of his followers. He smiled and said, "My life has finished, farewell to all of you". He was 75 years of age when he died in the February of Kanbun (1668). From these accounts it is apparent that he was a professional swordsman.

The type of blade that was used by this school, or the method of throwing is not really known. We can only guess this from the type used in the *Katōno-ryu*, the other name *Izu-ryu*, which seems to have been modelled on *Ganritsu* school. Assuming this, the shape of the blade and the way to throw it would be similar to '*Chokuda*' (straight throw), which I will mention later.

THE ORIGIN OF SHURIKEN – KATŌNO-RYU

There is a school which is part of the *Ganritsu-ryu* of Matsubayashi Henyasai and this is thought to be one of the representative schools of the *Shuriken* art in Japan.

The founder was Fujita Hirohide of Katōno who was a *samurai* of the *Sendai-han* and whose other name was to be Katōno Isu. So that is also called *Izu-ryu*. He learnt the arts of *Shuriken* and *Kendō* in the *Ganritsu-ryu* and was taught by Matsubayashi Henyasai and his best pupil Shindō Kanshiro. He pioneered the use of a needle in the *Shuriken* art. This needle which was 10cm in length and 20gm in weight, was thick at one end and originally employed in the making of the helmet, armour and leather mask. The '*Ōshu-hanashi*' written by Makuzujo, a daughter of Kudō Heisuke, a doctor of the *Sendai-han*, mentions him. 'It is said Katōno Izu served during Meiwa and Anei (1764-1780). He had mastered most aspects of military fighting techniques and was particularly adept in the art of *Shuriken*. He would hold a needle between his middle finger and forefinger and whenever he threw it, never missed his target. The original intention of this device was that on an encounter with the enemy if he blinded them at first there would be no further cause for fear. He was reputed to secretly keep needles constantly in his hair.

The lord before long allowed him to give demonstrations, offering the use of a picture of a horse standing under a cherry tree, painted on a Japanese cedar door. Izu, with great accuracy and using two needles at a time, could hit each hoof in turn.

This art developed and spread to the other han in the East – North of Japan

Kaiho Hanpei, especially, was an expert of this technique. He was the second master of the sword art at the *Hokushin Itto-ryu*, and was a member of the *Mito-han* during the last days of the Tokugawa Shogunate. Under his tuition there was a master swordsman, Neigishi Nobunori (Shorei) who came from the *Annaka-han* of Jōshu, who created a new school which came to be known as the *Negishi Shuriken-ryu*.

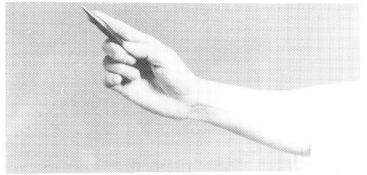

B – The method of holding a blade in Jikishin.

103

THE LITTLE LONG-NOSED GOBLIN OF JOSHŪ (NEGISHI RYU)

As I have mentioned before, the originator of the Negishi School was a retainer of Jōshū Annaka called Negishi Shorei. As a child he suffered from a weak disposition and was rather different from the other children. He would often hit or thrust the *Kendo* type faceguard on the lintels and pillars with a *shinai* (a bamboo sword). His parents noticed that his arm movements were extremely agile and they decided to have him taught the art of swordsmanship by a master so he would be properly trained. He enjoyed the art very much, and with enthusiam plus his natural ability, he progressed rapidly and soon became the greatest swordsman in his clan.

Afterwards, by order of his clan, he studied under the master of the *Mito-han*, Kaiho Hanpei, at the same time he went to Chiba Shusaku and Chiba Eijiro. In addition he also mastered the esoteric hereditary art of swordsmanship of the *Araki-ryū* and also the *Sō-jutsu* (spearmanship) of the *Oshima-ryu*. Finally he became the head of the *Kaiho-ryū*.

He was the head of the school for several years and since he had completely mastered the techniques he left his master. He visited *Sakuma Zozan* of Matsushiro Shinshū and then travelled around each of the clans of Ōshū. One year later he returned home to report the results of his mission. Then he became a master of the art of swordsmanship thus further enhancing his reputation. He was known as 'the long-nosed goblin of Jōshū'.

Eventually the feudal system in the divisions of the provinces was abolished and a new provisional system took its place. As soon as the order was announced, Negishi replaced his sword with a threshing tool and worked only on his farm. He passed away on the 15th July in Meiji 37 (1904) at the age of 65.

The *Negishi-ryu* was founded by Negishi Shorei. The blades used by this school weigh about 50 gm and are shaped like pencils but with slightly thicker points. There are many different shaped blades, for example hexagonal, octagonal, circular and the spear type. These blades have especially a distinctive tail part. It is adorned with tassles made from threads or fur from a bear or a horse. According to their length, weight and the additional tail part they are made for throwing a short distance, a middle distance and a long distance. These blades, especially the ones with fur tails, are unique in Japan as well as in other countries.

I'll point out the shurikens of the Negishi school as follows. A.B.C. without the tail are for throwing a short distance. D.E. are adorned with fur from the tail of horse and are for throwing to the middle distance. F.G.H. are rolled in with threads at the tail and are suitable for throwing a long distance. I.J.K. have tassles and are for throwing a short distance.

Above all, it is the characteristic of the Negishi school that the blades are adjusted according to the structure at the tail part for the various distances. The most important training and aim of this school is how to throw a long distance with a blade for a short distance.

In the case of making the blade of the Negishi school, especially the tail part, we thread a hole through the tail part of a blade with the hair of a horse's tail and roll them over hard, and again we roll them many times over it with threads, to finish we congeal it with lacquer.

The distance of the great hit is fixed according to air resistance at the length of the tail part. This is the reason why there is the important oral instruction of 'Enkin no Soku' 'Measurement of Far and Near'.

As I mentioned, the Negishi School designed the tail part of a blade so that it would fly directly for a long distance by controlling the turning of the blade. That is, they created blades for near, middle and far distances by changing the position of the centre of gravity with alterations in length and weight of the tail.

Besides these blades, there is a cross-shuriken which was developed centering around the Mito-han. Although I say a cross-shuriken, it is different from the cross-shuriken which was used by the Ninja, the Koga School and the Iga School as mentioned elsewhere. The shuriken, which was used by the feudal clan, Mitso, resembled a slender bomb in shape, and is cross-shaped at the tail part, like today's tail end of a bomb or a rocket bomb.

A Japanese shuriken is, needless to say, the originator of using a shuttlecock at the tail end of a bomb, since the cross shuriken was made long before the standard finned bomb used by aircraft.

There is a factual account, printed in the Tokyo Nichi Nichi News (now the Mainichi News) on the 19th May 1940, when the Second World War was at its height. A correspondent, Takamatsu, headlined his news report 'German Planes Use Shuriken', was followed by "A German plane attacked an English merchant ship, firing a shower of 3″ long steel arrows that killed and wounded many of the crew on the ship. They had revived the weapon used in the first world war which had the form of a *shuriken*, and which originated in Japan".

On the use of *shuriken* in Europe, the following story can be told about Lord Akitake, General Yoshinobo's younger brother, who was only 15 years old when he was sent on a mission to France in 1865 by the Tokugawa Bakufu (shogunate). Because he was given the important task of extending good will between the countries, and no one knew what might happen in a land that was completely unknown to them, guardians were carefully selected, and a cross *shuriken* expert from the *Mito-han* also joined the party.

The chosen attendant took a few *shurikens* with him, but had no need to use them in the peaceful city of Paris. On preparing to return home they gave the *shurikens* to several people, who had become their friends, as souvenirs. One such *shuriken* was exhibited at a Paris Military museum.

In the first World War, a French technical officer designed an arrow which could be thrown by hand, having got the idea from the *Shuriken*. When they dropped the arrows onto the German Army's troops, they were surprised to find that the result was greatly effective.

The arrows dropped by the French were 12cm in length, 8mm in diameter and weighed 15gm. Between 3500 and 4000 were loaded onto a plane and when the arrows were dropped from an altitude of 2000m they fell towards the ground at a speed of 150 metres per second; and at a height of 1000m they dropped at a speed of 100 metres per second.

The penetration was so great that the arrow was able to pierce through the shoulder of someone on horseback and continue straight into the body of the horse; thus it was able to kill and wound a man and his horse at the same time.

Later, the English army used this weapon also, changing the shape. The German army made one 13″ in length, patterning the base section of the arrow so that it would twist as it dropped. During the Second World War when all knowledge of modern science was being pressed into service, the *Shurikens* were continually in use. Whilst the Japanese themselves were unaware of the fact, the European sky was a battlefield between scientifically designed cross *shurikens* of both sides.

We often see the orginial Japanese idea expressed in the shape of the modern aeroplane and the rocket. Not only can one note a resemblance in modern day space craft to the original style of the Japanese, but even the more futuristic missiles and planes bear that same resemblance to the *shuriken*. Old things do not always die.

I am convinced that the Japanese art of *shuriken* will inspire many inventions in the future. Whilst I was investigating the art of throwing objects, and the various methods employed by people of all ages from different countries, I became convinced that there is only one fundamental theory involved, and that the Japanese *Shuriken* art not only includes the whole of this theory but also possesses a characteristic which is not found in any other throwing arts. It can be said therefore that the Japanese *Shuriken* is the superior of all of the throwing arts of the world.

THE FINE TECHNIQUES OF THE TURNING HIT – (SHIRAI-RYŪ)

The founder of the Shirai Ryo was Toro Yoshikane a clansman of the Okayama-han. He was born in third year of *Tenmei* (1782) and was a well known swordsman during the last days of the Tokugawa shogunate.

The blade used in this school was 25cm long and shaped like tongs (similar to those used to put pieces onto a charcoal fire). This school's technique of throwing is representative of those using the turning hit method, which turns once in the air and hits the target, and not the direct hit method used in the *Negishi-ryū* and the *Katori-shinto-ryū*. But, when throwing up to a distance of approximately 2.7m, they use the direct hit method, since it is difficult to turn a blade once in the air before reaching the target. The shape of the blade is very simple with no decoration on the tail part and of consistent thickness. Concerning the type of stance: they hold the *shuriken* with the point facing oneself but a few *shurikens* are held in the shape of a fan with the left hand in front of the left cheek of the face and each one is taken with the right hand and lightly thrown from the shoulder. This feat of throwing 'lightly' is very difficult to achieve. If any extra power is added to the blade it will turn too much and will not hit the target. If, however, we remove a quarter of the power of the blade, it will not spin very much and the blade will be powerless. After going through many hardships, at last even if we throw the blade using all our strength, it spins moderately and strikes the target strongly. Your feeling as the blade hits the target is impossible to describe. The feeling is entirely different from the direct throw. After the throw the person should concentrate solely on the target with the palm of the hand stretched out so it is parallel to the face.

Well then I illustrate the flying state of the blade of the Negishi School and the Shirai School as follows.

However, as before mentioned, the founder of the *Shirai-ryū Shuriken* art was Shirai Toru Yoshikane, but more about him later. Now I will write about Kurokawa Naiden Gorō Kanenori who was a representative swordsman of this school.

He had mastered the technique so skillfully that from a distance of 5m he was able to pierce a hole in a coin which he was using as his target. He excelled in the swordsmanship of the *Jinmuso-Itto-ryū, Jujitsu* of the *Inakamishinmiyo-ryū*, and in the art of *Naginata* (a halberd) of the *Sei-ryū, Anazawa-ryū*; but he was exceptionally skilful at the *Shirai Shuriken-ryū*.

At one time he had a *dojo*. According to the educational council of the *Aizu-han*, *shuriken* is written 'Senken' (iron tool or implement) and about the shape of the *shuriken* and the way to throw it, it is described as follows. "You hold the nail-like object that is about 21cm long in the right hand by the shoulder and throw it as you step forward".

Although in his later years he lost his sight due to an eye disease, he never gave up his lessons. It was said that he hung an 18cm board on a pillar after groping around it, walked backwards about 5.50, and he was able to strike the target every time.

His eldest son was killed in the *Boshin battle* (1868) in Aizu and his second son came home from the battle wounded. Repressing his tears, he killed his dear son who was completely crippled. He then killed himself with the same sword. He was 65 years old.

陰剣　　陰剣　　手裏剣

剣の装着の仕方

137　手裏剣術の基本型　　　2. Wearing shuriken.

THE DESPERATE STRUGGLE AGAINST A SICKLE AND CHAIN (ENMEI-RYU)

The *Enmei-ryu* was founded by Miyamoto Musashi. Part of the inscription of the Buddhist monument of a priest, Shunzan, who was the chief priest of Lord Hosoka-wa's family temple of Kumamoto in Higo, is connected with *Shuriken* and it says of Musashi: "As he lets fly a blade, or throws a wooden blade escapees and runners cannot flee. The blade has power as if it has been fired from a strong catapult, and never missed its target. Even *Yoyū, an expert archer in China, was not able to better him."*

The '*Nitenki*' tells us that a man who was known as Shishido was an expert with a *kusari-gama*. He fought Miyamoto Musashi. As Shishido shook out his chain, Musashi threw a dagger and struck it through Shishido's chest, killing him instantly. From this we can see that in combat with a swordsman, the throwing blade can beat the sword. It seems that the blade used throwing was usually made suitably fine and balanced.

Even now it is said that amongst the *kata* of *kumikomi* (forms of armour grappling) or swordsmanship in the *Negishi-ryū* there is the *kata* with which Musashi fought. That is we take the position with a *shuriken* in the right hand and vertically hold up a *tachi* in the left hand. After having hit with the *shuriken* we attach the right hand to the *tachi*, and then take the posture of *Hasso-no kamae*. And the other one is to take the posture with a *tachi*, which is held in the left hand, at the right side. This *kamae* prevents the blade from being caught by a chain.

In the memoirs of Watanabe Kōan called 'Koan Taiwa', it says: "Yoemon, the son of Takemura Musashi (Kōan usually called him this), is an expert swordsman of the same calibre as his father. He was also skilled in the art of *shuriken*. Once he set a peach afloat on a river and threw a 40cm sword at it. The sword pierced through the centre of the peach..."

From this story it should be noted that the length of the sword is stated expressly. Also from the description it is interesting that he set the peach afloat on the river and took aim at a moving target. You can see that Musashi and the students of his school were trained to throw daggers.

In the *Edo* period the well known *Shuriken* experts were Miyamoto Musashi of the *Enmei-ryū* and his adopted son Takemura Yoemon Tsunenori, in his case it was especially called the *Takemura-ryū*. A disciple of the *Takemura-ryū*, Iijima Hyōbei took this art to its completion. It was inherited from Hyōbei to Dogen Tasaemon, from Niki Juemon to Asano Denemon, finishing with Tanba Orie ujinaga. This is the *Chishin-ryū* of Shuriken art.

The *Shosho-ryū* also shaped their blades in dagger fashion.

The throwing dagger of the Imperial Guard, Ogasawara Tadamasa, Lord of the Kokura Castle of Kyushu, is mentioned as having the same style as the one mentioned above. He was also an expert in the *shuriken* art of dagger throwing. 'Ōsaka Gunki' (Ōsaka military discipline) states that he threw a short sword as if it were a *shuriken*. Some of the blades were adorned with tassles at the ends (see illustration).

THE AMAZING SKILLS OF THROWING 36 SHURIKEN REPEATEDLY (THE MŌRI-RYŪ)

It is said that Mōri Gentarō Gentatsu was the originator of the *Mōri-ryū*. In listing the stories of this legendary biography I came across the following:

Mōri Gentatsu was the son of Kikyōya, a timber dealer who owned a wholesale shop in Yokobori of Ōsaka. His given name was Gentaro and he was raised by a wealthy family. He was a cripple but there are conflicting stories as to how he became a cripple; some say he was born a cripple, some that he was afflicted with gout in his childhood, and others say he was injured by lumber which fell down onto his foot. At all events, since he was not able to go out because of his disability, he would pass away the time by furtively attempting to catch sparrows by throwing 15cm nails at the birds.

Finally he achieved this skill in his own way having developed another kind of *shuriken*.

Holding 36 nails, 18 in each hand, he was able to throw them continuously, as he moved them quickly in his hand. It seems that he used either a 15cm nail or a blade of the same size; he did not use the thick blade of the *Negishi-ryū*. As his military name became more renowned, he changed his name to Mōri Gentatsu. Whilst he was a *Musha-shugyōsha*, wandering in search of adventure, he challenged Yagyu Jubei, who was in the camp of Masakizaka of Yamato, to a match. I will mention this match between the swordsmen later. Despite his unfortunate birth and handicapped child-hood, you can see that he strived to master the special art. To this day many people will recollect having practised throwing these 15cm nails when they were children.

短刀型手裏剣

Tanto gata shuriken.
(A short sword shaped shuriken).

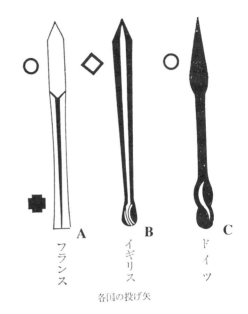

A
フランス

B
イギリス

C
ドイツ

各国の投げ矢

Throwing arrows from various countries.
A – France, B – England, C – Germany

手裏剣として使用された笄

Kōgai used as shuriken.

THE SHURIKEN OF KŌGAI – AN ORNAMENTAL HAIR-PIN (THE SHOSETSU-RYŪ)

This is the school of Yui Minbe no Suke Tachibana Shōsetsu and other people who belong to that school.

It is written in 'Kobunko' by Dr. Mozume that "Yui Shosetsu was admitted as a *Shuriken* expert and at the time there was no one else like him in the world": however, the shape of his *shuriken* and his way of throwing it are not mentioned.

In 'Kinsei Jitsuroko Zenshū', the complete works of the modern authentic record, edited by Dr. Tsubouchi there is a story of Shosetsu when he fought with Sekiguchi Hayato, who was an expert in *Iai-jutsu and responsible to the Kii-han* for its instruction, telling how Shosetsu threw a Kogai (hair-pin) instead of a *shuriken*. It should be noted that at the time, Sekiguchi Hayato was a martial arts expert, the whole country being familiar with his name, and that Shosetsu was a strategist who was skilled in the 18 martial arts.

One day, while in the service of the Lord Kii Dainagon Yorinori, they had to fight to the finish using *Iai-jutsu* by his Lord's command. They stood in the centre of the *Dōjo* wearing the 85cm swords. Sevvereal hundred students of Sekiguchi were looking at him steadily with suppressed excitement because if Hayato was beaten it would bring shame onto the Tokugawa family.

The two combatants stood glaring at each other with their hands on the *Tsuba* (sword-guard) of their swords, then at the same instant they both moved and their swords struck together. Shosetsu moved back about 5m, whilst Hayato, thinking that here was his chance, ran up to him with a flourish of his sword, only to fall as the *kogai* which Shosetsu had thrown pinned his *hakama* (pleated skirt) to the floor of the *Dōjo*; the throw was so rapid as to have been unperceived.

The main point to be noted in this story is that Shosetsu threw a *kogai* as a *shuriken*. Since he was a careful person, it is thought that he disguised a well-balanced *shuriken* to resemble a *kogai*.

THE DESPERATE SWORD (KATORI-SHINTO-RYŪ)

The founder of the *Shinto-ryū* was Iishino Choisai and this school is representative of Kenjutsu in the East of Japan. It is thought that the art of *shuriken* was studied as one

十字手裏剣の持ち方

The way of holding a shuriken

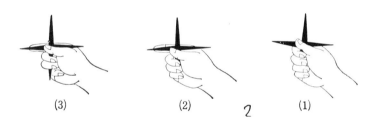

(3)　　　　　　(2)　　2　　(1)

The way of holding shuriken

用意周到な正宇のことであるから、筆と見せて、実は均衡の理にかなった手裏剣である

香取神道流の手裏剣

たとえられる。

Shuriken of Katori shinto-ryu.

part of the course of the *waza* (technique) of swordsmanship.

The blade of this school that is handed down today looks like a square *hashi* (chopstick), but some people say that they threw a dagger, and the following account confirms this:

One of the distinctions of this school is the way the blade is thrown. At the moment the blade is thrown, the person should take a step forward to give the impression of a frontal attack. The other distinction concerns the length of the blade. When attacking and throwing a blade, the length of the blade is determined by the *maai* distance, it is to be thrown; so in order to prevent continual changing of the blade, at the risk of your life, advance to the right distance with a fixed blade. These distinctions show the typical spirit of the Japanese Martial Arts.

THE SHURIKEN OF A 'NINJITSU' PRACTITIONER (CROSS SHAPED, EIGHT SIDED SHURIKEN)

The cross *shuriken* was used by practitioners of *ninjitsu* at the *Koga-ryū* or *Iga-ryū*. It was a cross shaped *shuriken* that had a blade pointing out in four directions. There was another cross shaped *shuriken* with a blade pointing in eight directions. A further type looked like a sword, but as it was opened was in fact a cross-shaped *shuriken*. This was thrown end over end at the enemy. I often see, on the television or films, a *shuriken* thrown horizontally in error. The cross *shuriken* spins during flight and because of the four points it has a greater chance of piercing the target and is ideal for both short or long distances. But there are fatal weak points to this blade. It is easily dodged and its flight stopped by an enemy, and because the resistance to the air is great, the speed is slow and the area through which it spins is large.

According to Buddhist legend, one origin of the cross *shuriken* is found in *Hōrin* (in Buddhism). There was once a king who ruled the world not with the power of the sword, but with the spinning *shuriken* 'Rimpho'. After that this Rimpho was called 'Horin', its shape resembles to the helm of a ship. The story says that once he took Rimpho and threw it with such force that it broke everything it touched into pieces, including a mountain rock. It is interesting to note that this weapon originated from a religious ornament.

There are various shaped *shuriken* of this type. Although it is an ancient weapon the design is very interesting from the point of view of modern design. Representative ones are here shown illustrated.

Very few people know what I have mentioned regarding the method of throwing a cross *shuriken*. In TV or film, people throw a Cross shuriken horizontally, which is wrong. It should be thrown vertically holding a blade as in the illustration.

114

RYOTAN-NO-MAYOI (WOVEN AT BOTH ENDS)

I had learned *Negishi-ryu* and *Shirai-ryu* under Master Naruse and I had looked into other schools as much as possible. But I began to think that I would like to create my own technique of *shuriken* in my life time. (Not only a *shuriken* as an object but 'the world of myself' through *shuriken* and the technique). A strong element in my mind about this was a legend that Inei, who was a founder of the *Yari* technique of the Hozōin-ryu, based his own *Kama-yari* on the crossed shape of a half-moon and his spear which he saw reflected in the surface of a pond.

Inei was a monk of Hōzō temple which belonged to the Kegon sect. He became an expert by training himself with a spear in the temple garden. In his mind he felt that the most important thing was not only the proficiency in the art of the spear but also the unity of himself and the spear. The complete unity of weapon and person; subject and object; ascetic and the active; thought and behaviour. This unity of mind is called '*Sanmai*' in Buddhism. '*Sanmai*' was the real purpose of this hard training.

One night he noticed that a spearhead which was twinkling in a pond crossed the reflection of the new moon in the water. The truth of '*Sanmai*' burst upon him. The shape which embodied the idea was '*Kama-yari*' (sickle-spear) of the *Hoẑōin-ryū*... the shape of the new moon fixed at the spearhead.

It seemed to me that the Japanese swordsmen and the technique ended by creating an individual world through each technique. 'My own *shuriken*' does not necessarily mean any unusual shape of *shuriken*, but the finding of a new world in myself.

In the *Negishi-ryū*, we put everything on one straight line and let the movement of whole parts of our body suffice. It is the best technique from the point of view that the blade is an individual expression of modern aerodynamics theory. But the weak point is that the blade is too artificial. There are different blades for short distance, middle distance and long distance. That is, one blade will not suffice. Good for aiming at a still target, it is faulty when aiming at a foe in movement. On the other hand, one can use the blade of the *Shirai-ryū* for any distance and one's ingenuity is not taxed, but this way of throwing is not as effective as the *Negishi-ryū*. In particular, the fatal fault of the *Shirai-ryū* is the way in which we hold the point of a blade forward for throwing at a near distance; for a middle distance we have at once to shift a blade end-point forward for changing to the turning hit. Since one dares not be off guard in front of the enemy even for a moment, it would be a fatal fault to shift a blade thus. Was there no way of throwing which overcame the faults of both *Shirai* and the *Negishi-ryū*? Couldn't I create an art which used the advantages of both schools? I did not think that it would be easy to unite them, I still wanted to establish 'a secure blade' which united the advantage of the two schools.

I tried this and that, but with no success. I realised that here were two worlds, each with a strict limit.

I stood between the direct hit and the turning hit. I could devote myself fully to neither, nor could I make any peace between them. How, I wondered did our ancestors think about it? How would they have thought? It was not a question I would have thought to ask my master in his lifetime. How did the schools think about it? I wondered if I were probably wrong to think such a thing. At all events, my own thoughts were getting me nowhere. But one day, without knowing why, I threw a blade of the *Shirai-ryū* in the way of the *Negishi-ryū* and there was my solution. 'Throw a blade of the *Shirai-ryū* in the posture of the *Negishi-ryū*.

THE WORLD OF IKKU

A combination of the posture of the *Negishi-ryū* and the blade of the *Shirai-ryū* shows a strong flight and strike. But in the investigation of this new way of hitting, there was a difficult problem about what to do to 'shift a blade'. It means that there is no way to change from near distance to long distance without shifting the blade. As long as this problem was unsolved, I couldn't solve 'the both ends' (*Shirai-ryū* or *Negishi-ryū*) the direct hit or the turning hit. Again I fell to thought, and one day, the Zen word came to my help.

'*Ryōtō-o-Tomoni Saidanshi Ikken Ten-ni Yotte Samushi*'

This is as follows:

Before Kusunoki Masashinge fell fighting in the Minatogawa battle, he practiced *Zen* meditation in Kōgen Temple in Hyōgo province with the monk Sōchu Myōgoku who came from China. During his preparation for the last battle he asked the monk, "What shall I do at the time when in a battle?" The master of *Zen* replied, "Ryōtō-o-tomoni Saidanshi Ikken Ten-ni Yotte Samushi" ("Cut off both the heads and feel refreshed as if a sword firmly stands in the sky") – clearly overcomes both ends, victory or defeat, life or death, charge in fresh feeling as if a sword stands in the sky – these words also mean the ultimate state in *Zen*, I think.

116

By the words "cut off both ends" I was inspired to cut off both the ends of a *shuriken*. Then, I fixed an edge at the *Shirai* blade at the edgeless end which doesn't have the edge. Thus, it now had edges at the front or rear. There was in fact no difference between the front and rear: it was no longer a *Shirai-ryū* blade. I threw, and it stuck well.

Thus, the 'problem of both ends' vanished, along with '*Negishi-ryū* or *Shirai-ryū*, '*the direct hit or the turning hit*' and '*The artificial blade or the natural blade*'.

The blade should be thrown in the method of the direct hit at near distances, and at long distances it should be thrown with the turning hit of the *Shirai-ryū*. You need not shift the blade because there is no difference between the front and the rear. This was a completely new world, and I had made it. You can talk of blades and how to throw them, but for me, the result of my ten years' work had ended at last in the creation of 'the world of my own blade'.

In this state there was no division between the way of throwing and the shape of the blade. The end-result of so much pulling about between one way and another was that I reached the simple state in which I forgot myself and simply threw the blade. I think this had a lot to do with the fact that I was interested in *Zen* from my boyhood. Of '*Ken-Zen Ichi*', I always thought that they were originally different ways, but the points they had in common enabled one to help the other.

In fact, I now realised the true meaning of '*Zen-Ken Ichi*', that is, they are completely one. I have named this approach which I have just described '*Ikku-ryū*' and I continue to strive for the true '*mind*' and '*waza*' of this school.

So much for *shuriken*, but what is the ultimate end? When I look back upon the past and think of my future goals, I can say this: First of all, you have to reach and gain the basic *Kata*, commune with your own blade, be able to throw any object as if it were the best blade, attune yourself to any space and be able to throw a blade freely in any situation. Then we have to go on to the next state in which we have thrown away the all without losing the above-mentioned state. The state in which we should be able to throw any object as if it were the finest blade implies that all things around us have become *shurikens*. To quote the 11th article of '*Itto-ryū Heihō Mokuroku*' by Itō Ittōsai written towards the end of his life, '*Ban Butsu Mikata-no-Koto*' ('everything is a friend'). If we want to be sure of victory, why use only a sword or blade? In an emergency, if we take any tea caddy or a kettle which happens to hand and throw it, we can break an enemy's spirit. All things come to your hand if you have the spirit. This

117

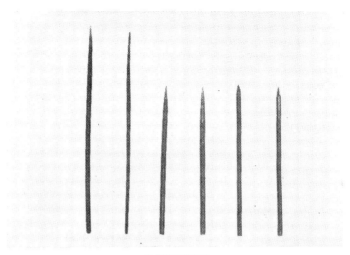

白井流の手裏剣

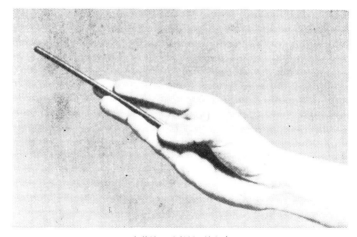

白井流の手裏剣の持ち方

65 手裏剣術の歴史と流派

A. Shuriken of the Shirai-ryu.
B. The way of holding a shuriken of the Shirai-ryu.

refs to a state in which we should be able to throw everything as a superb weapon, it reminds me of the story of Miyamoto Musashi in his late life. When Musashi was looking at the rising of the moon over a mountain as he was sitting on a verandah on a summer evening, one of his students thought to test his master's expertise in swordsmanship. He struck at the master from the rear with a *bokken*, or wooden sword. Simultaneously, Musashi easily dodged, and pulled the mat on the verandah, so that the student tripped and fell. Musashi continued to look innocently at the moon. There was no sword, no victory or defeat, but only the fact that Musashi was looking at the moon. In *shuriken*, I must also reach this state. To sum up 'All truth is *Ikku* (freedom from all worldly thoughts), examine it with care' as mentioned at the end of '*Gorinosho*'. There are many ways but the way that leads to the end is only a sword of *Ikku*.

Really, we should not talk and write about art. The more we talk, the more the truth fades away. Master Naruse used to admonish me when I reasoned too much, with an old song: '*Ki wa Waza ni, Ariake to Koso Omoekashi, Shōji Akereba, Tsuki wa Sasunari*'. 'If you think that a pale moon has risen, open the paper screen and the moon will shine in'. There is nothing to understand about wanting to see the moon, even if we talk about the moonlight without opening the paper screen. We have to understand that the truth is in *waza* itself, total involvement and alertness.

TRAINING DIARY

THE TRAINING RECORD OF SHURIKEN

I recorded my experience and my thoughts about the training of *shuriken* every day and called it '*Shuriken Shudorōku*' (The Training Record of *Shuriken*). I would like to quote from a few entries:

'Today I faced great difficulty. I could not make my way to even one step. A target, a blade, feet, the right hand and the left hand were all on one line. Ideally the blade flies on a straight line, but the blade went out to the right and left. There is trouble in the way I throw a blade by changing a turning movement of my waist to a straight line movement. Isn't it possible? When I think of the straight line, the blade deflects but when I throw it without thinking, it flies straight. This may be the gateway to being free of all worldly thoughts. Always train hard and make an effort to throw a blade being free of worldly thoughts in any case.' Why did I train in this art? There was a note about it as follows:

'From my childhood, I saw what was right and often wanted to do it. But I thought that I was powerless and good for nothing as a man so I did not do it. I regretted this in my heart very much as I wanted to become strong and I trained my mind and body. I wanted to learn the martial arts, but my body could not bear the hard training and I was in mental distress. One day, I suddenly became aware of *shuriken*. This art is not in general well accepted and in former times was considered a rather cowardly act. Cowardice is not in the art, but in the heart of the artist. I will train my heart and soul through this art and establish the true way of *shuriken*. Even if someone is an expert in *Kendo* (swordsmanship), *jujutsu* and spear fighting when I am at a distance from him, he cannot do anything to me. This is the most effective distance. I am lucky! I am aware of this art.'

And the other day...

'A blade; threw it out in a straight line cutting through from the forehead to the body.'

'A blade: It is because the right foot is in the wrong position that a blade swings to the left and the right. Be careful!'

'If the mind is not right, the blade is also not right.'

'No power, power!'

'I felt this keenly after my training with *shuriken*'.

'If there is worry in the heart, the blade becomes a worried blade. The flying state is as if it is a fallen leaf in the storm.'

'If there is in the heart the intent to show off, the blade is also thrown in vain.'

'If the heart is calm and the mind is right, the blade is like a flash of lightening that goes a great distance: the power is as strong as if it could pierce through a giant rock.'

As my heart became more and more calm, my mind became settled. In hard training, my mind was usually occupied by '*Tachigiri sen yon hyaku men*' (fight against 1400 opponents without taking mask off) which was done at the Yamaoka Teshu Koji *dojo*.

This was the match of Tachigiri: 1400 fights in seven days, when a student who trained over five years under this '*Dojo*' asked to take a 'vow'. What was said to be the most wonderful state was that the Tachigiri fighting lost thought of mind and body, reached his 'true heart' around two or three o'clock in the afternoon each day.

During the Tachigiri period of seven days the *Tachigirisha* was not allowed out and was only allowed to eat rice gruel, so his desperate fight was beyond description. His limbs and his whole body swelled up, and there were often a few people who passed bloody urine. Every day after his match he had to go in front of *Koshi*, kneel and bow low which was not easy in the circumstances, so he was reproved for his timidness by *Koshi*. Even those students who were thought to be cowards by *Koshi* were feared as King of the Lions by swordsmen of other schools. An outline of his instruction of the vow follows:–

'When the way of the sword becomes real, it decides life and death. At present, the way of the sword is thought of as a game. Fighting declines into a matter of victory or defeat and I cannot see power as witnessed in a real fight. So in our *Dōjō*, we do severe training. We try to fight to the last hit without losing our spirit. We demand to be trained for the real fight.'

AN EXPERIMENT WITH SHURIKEN AND A NEW SCHOOL

THE ESSENCE OF THE BOOMERANG

It is generally thought that the boomerang's journey to and from the thrower's hand draws a circle, but in fact it draws an arc (see illustration 1). Some believe also that it should be thrown to the side keeping it level with the ground, but that is not the correct way. One should throw it up at about 45° to 60° holding it at right angles to the ground, and just when the boomerang is about to leave the hand, twist it a little and this gives it its spinning power. Try to make it fly level, and it will because the boomerang always rises to one side. Because of the little twist we have given it, as it rises and reaches a certain distance it turns its position from vertical to horizontal.

FUJIGATA ICHIGO 'HIRAIKEN', FUJI SHAPED THE FIRST 'FLYING SWORD'

My purpose in researching the boomerang was to clarify the mystery about it and to refute an established world theory that the Australian boomerang is the only returning article in the world. I learned that there are many parallel methods and theories that could rightly be called the Japanese *Shuriken* Art. The Australian natives' posture when preparing himself to throw, as in the pictures, is clearly '*Koso no Kamae*' (the facing phase posture).

The next step was to do my best to create a completely new style of boomerang with a better performance, but on the basis of the Japanese *shuriken*.

I made several kinds of boomerang, at least ten different types, and I kept putting them to the test. At that time my office was in Otemachi, and in the lunch break I would often try the boomerang *shuriken* out in the Imperial Plaza. About ten years ago anyone who was taking a walk in the Imperial Plaza was bound to see me, looking very serious, throwing various types of wooden objects high into the sky. In this place, we are strictly forbidden to play ball or walk on the grass. The Imperial Police patrolmen often came but my missile wasn't a ball and flew over the grass but never fell on it – since it always came back to me – so he could not forbid me to do it, and just watched my test, at a loss. I finally concluded that the cross *shuriken* style is the best of the Japanese *shuriken*.

Three years later I completed the boomerang *Fuji-Gata-dai-ichi-Go* in the Japanese style which flew well and returned accurately, even better than the Australian boomerang. I named the Japanese style boomerang *Hiraiken* which means a flying, coming back sword. I showed this to Madame Dorothy Bennet who is well known as an investigator of Australian primitive culture, when she came to Japan at the invitation of the Yomiuria newspaper company. I threw it six times and caught it each time, right in front of her. The lady was surprised when she saw it and told me "I suppose there are only a few people left who can correctly throw and catch the boomerang, for the natives who know the art have nearly all died out. Soon all knowledge of it will disappear. Many boomerangs are made for the tourists, but they are all imitation. Not only are they non-returning but they do not fly properly either. The article which you made is a completely different style to ours, but the precision of return is wonderful." I presented her with a small red, yellow and green *Hiraiken* as a souvenir.

Many would laugh and question the use of this in our busy modern world. Well, I would like to challenge the greatest expert of Australian Boomerang throwing to a match, to be arranged through their embassy. If this challenge be accepted I will happily and calmly turn up on the day with a super large-sized *Hiraiken* constructed along the lines of the traditional theory of Japanese *Shuriken*.

The flying course of the Boomerang.

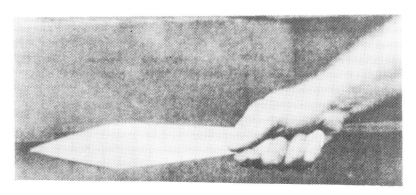

124

A POST SCRIPT

In closing this book I would like to say thank you to the following masters: Master Naruse who taught me about the art of *shuriken* of the *Negishi* and *Shirai-ryū*; Master Fiujita Saiko of the head family of the *Ninjutsu Koga-ryū* and the *Shingetsu-ryū* of *shuriken* art; and Master Miyamura Chizuka who taught me *Kyujutsu* (bow and arrow technique), *Uchi-ne,* and *Yadome* art.

Signed Shirakami Ikku-ken

SHURIKEN AS A DEFENCE ART

1. Even the weak can use *shuriken* for self-defence. Women and old people for example, can make good use of it.
2. *Shuriken* is silent.
3. It can attack the enemy from a distance, while he cannot retaliate.
4. With *shuriken*, you can attack rapidly and continuously.
5. You can carry a *shuriken* at all times and places.
6. You can discourage an enemy from attacking without having to kill him.
7. According to your progress in *Waza*, your spirit becomes stronger until at last you can defeat an enemy without even having to fight him.

THE INSTRUCTION OF SHURIKEN

1. We must fully realise that *shuriken* is a sacred art and a sacred weapon; we should not use it save in a just cause.
2. We should not use it for a quarrel, a private grudge, for hunting, or otherwise killing small creatures.
3. We should not be fascinated by victory or defeat, or compete with other people for *Waza*.
4. We should not teach the art of *shuriken* to a man of evil disposition.
5. We should not train except in an open place, clear of spectators.
6. Nor in any public place.

THE EFFECT OF SHURIKEN

1. In *Shuriken* training, the mind becomes calm as we banish worldly thoughts.
2. As long as the mind is not calm, a blade cannot be thrown correctly.
3. *Shuriken* aids mental concentration.
4. *Shuriken* teaches perseverance because unless we learn the basic training step by step, we shall not advance towards mastering the art.
5. Distractions will be banished, because when we are throwing a blade, we are free from worldly thoughts.
6. We are not frightened by force and we gain confidence in ourselves.
7. As we progress, in power, the mind loses its attachment to violence.

AN OUTLINE OF THE WRITER'S CAREER

Born in 1921 in Tokyo.
Graduated from the faculty of literature, Waseda University in 1947.
Taught at Jiyūgaoka High School. After that, engaged in foreign trade. Interested in the *shuriken* since boyhood. He was taught swordsmanship of the *Hokushin-Itto-ryū* by his uncle, General Hayashi Senjuro and *Heki-ryu,* archery and the *uchine* art by another uncle, Miyamura Chizuka. He studied under the master of the *shuriken* art, Naruse Kanji of the head family of the *Negishi-ryū*. Initiated into the mysteries of the *Negishi-ryu* and the *Shirai-ryu Shuriken* art in 1938.
Established the *shuriken* art of the *Ikku-ken* in 1965.
At present researching the martial arts of throwing.